Self-Study Approaches and the Teacher-Inquirer

Self-Study Approaches and the Teacher-Inquirer

Instructional Situations Case Analysis, Critical Autobiography, and Action Research

Hanna Ezer
Levinsky College of Education, Israel

Foreword by Naama Sabar Ben-Yehoshua

SENSE PUBLISHERS
ROTTERDAM/BOSTON/TAIPEI

A C.I.P. record for this book is available from the Library of Congress.

ISBN 978-90-8790-790-7 (paperback)
ISBN 978-90-8790-791-4 (hardback)
ISBN 978-90-8790-792-1 (e-book)

Published by: Sense Publishers,
P.O. Box 21858, 3001 AW
Rotterdam, The Netherlands
http://www.sensepublishers.com

Printed on acid-free paper

TABLE OF CONTENTS

TEACHERS' SELF STUDY, IDENTITY AND THE QUALITATIVE PARADIGM

In my capacity as an interpretive narrative researcher, I aspire to raise the level of professionalism among teachers through the rational and coherent use of qualitative research tools. Hence, I see a direct connection between qualitative interpretive research in education and self-study, the topic of this book written by Hanna Ezer, my former student and creative colleague.

The years I have spent engaged in qualitative research and in studying its impact on teacher education have underlined my belief that the qualitative research paradigm is an important tool in the hands of teacher-researchers and one that facilitates professional development among teachers. Self-study is situated in the interface between qualitative research as a tool in professional development among teachers and their search for a professional identity. As such, it enhances both professional development and professional identity. Indeed, self-study changes the way in which teachers think, for it leads them to move from intuitive and sometimes emotional thinking to systematic and rational thinking based on evidence. Hence, a teacher's professional identity is significant, primarily because the very act of forming an identity leads to a refinement of personal perceptions of the profession. In turn, this refinement itself constitutes a first step in becoming a professional.

In *The Jewish-Israeli voyage: Culture and identity* (2006)[1], Avi Sagi asserts that professional identity develops along a continuum of three layers. It begins with a layer of vague acquaintance with the professional self, continues through a layer of identification with the profession, and ultimately reaches a layer of knowledge, which involves conscious recognition of both the theoretical and the practical aspects of the profession. Sagi calls this recognition "connections of meaning." In the domain of the professional identity of teachers, "connections of meaning" are the fields of knowledge that construct teachers' professionalism, as, for example, education and values, pedagogy, knowledge of curriculum and expertise within the discipline. These stages of professional identity development are not necessarily sequential and can develop simultaneously.

In other words, the development of a professional identity is not a linear process. Indeed, professional development is dynamic and not static, and the range of knowledge utilized by educators in their teaching practice is in effect multidisciplinary and difficult to compartmentalize. As such, the teaching profession is characterized by complex situations. Moreover, it is difficult to let go of existing practices and acquire new ones, especially since teaching practices are often personal and idiosyncratic. As a result, in order to examine the practices characteristic of the teaching profession, the teacher-researcher must adapt the research philosophy and its tools to the studied situation and the goals of the study.

In the ongoing debate over the use of different research paradigms— for instance, the quantitative and qualitative paradigms—it appears that qualitative methods have established themselves firmly in education research. Structured tools, as required by the positivist (quantitative) paradigm, force the research into an existing schema, an enclosed, encapsulated situation, resulting in compression and closure as opposed to openness. On the other hand, qualitative tools attempt to open and reveal, to discover and to continue to search. Furthermore, it is the qualitative paradigm with its various traditions that offers the teacher-researcher engaged in self-study a variety of tools that can be used according to the teacher's own preferences and conditions. According to Bakhtin, for example, narrative research makes use of personal, internal discourse that speaks in a number of voices and brings to light misgivings and indecision. It is not authoritative, but rather examines, inquires, wonders and hesitates to some degree. As such, narrative research is appropriate for teachers curious to learn first of all about themselves and then about the background of their students and thus to find appropriate solutions to the problems. Such teachers can make use of the tradition of narrative research as self-study applied to their own teaching environment.

Ethnographic research, for its part, nurtures the skills of observation and attentiveness. It makes possible the cross-referencing of information and the sharpening of sensitivity, and it facilitates flexibility of thinking and openness to the unique qualities of the students. This sensitivity and openness allow for the development of teaching methods that are tailored to teaching situations based upon knowledge, caring and a sense of responsibility toward the students. In this research tradition, too, teacher-inquirers can adopt research skills such as observation and attentiveness to use in their own self-study.

Interpretive research, which seeks to examine and understand the perceptions and interpretations of the research subjects, provides the teacher with an appropriate tool for studying the school setting. In order to take the right action and to attain deeper and more useful understanding, it is therefore essential to utilize observation and attentiveness, and no less important, to clarify meanings as they are understood by the research subjects, whether they are the teachers themselves or their students.

A research genre that allows the researcher to study change and simultaneously test ways to effect change is action research. This genre provides the teacher a tool to watch the class closely, systematically and in real time and to observe a complex situation in which there are many variables that can neither be isolated nor controlled. On the basis of these in-class observations, the teacher-researcher can suggest a new method of action and also test it.

Hence it appears that various qualitative research traditions offer the teacher-researcher tools that involve observation, paying attention to others and to the self as well, posing questions and gathering rational interpretations with regard to complex teaching-learning situations. All these tools enhance teacher professionalism and contribute to establishing professional identity.

Identity is not an entity that can always be delineated. In fact, the study of identity covers a range of identities, for the individual is always simultaneously engaged in examining more than one identity. Hence, the tools appropriate for developing a professional identity are process-driven and open-ended. Conceived and designed throughout the course of the research, these tools allow for modifying the research questions according to developments within the research scenario. Further, they permit the researcher to observe complex teaching practice situations. These situations are made up of different kinds of knowledge that are not easily broken down into separate factors. Due to the complexity of teaching situations, then, it is reasonable to encourage teachers to investigate teaching situations they themselves have experienced by means of sensitive research tools from the domain of qualitative research, tools which will facilitate in-depth observation of complex teaching situations and will generate new knowledge and significant insights for the practitioner.

Ironically, those same dimensions of the qualitative paradigm that positivist methodologists object to are what constitute the advantages of the qualitative paradigm and its research tools. That is to say, those very elements of the qualitative paradigm that are "soft," less rigid and somewhat flexible constitute its strong points for the teacher-researcher. For when one seeks to construct an identity, which in the initial stages is unclear, searching, hesitant, difficult to describe precisely in terms of boundaries and contours, and which is cyclical and constantly changing as well, what is needed is a research tool that shares these same characteristics. These tools, then, are the research tools of the qualitative paradigm, tools that are built and take form during the course of the research and the picture emerging from it.

Hanna Ezer's book makes an important contribution to the literature in the field of defining and developing a professional identity. Most of the theoretical literature in this field discusses what the teacher should do. This book, in contrast, describes and analyzes what the teacher does.

Naama Sabar Ben-Yehoshua
Tel-Aviv University, 2008

ACKNOWLEDGEMENTS

I am privileged and honored to have been the teacher-educator guiding these attentive and scholarly teachers who went back to school and plunged into the deep water as novice researchers. Over my years of teaching, I have witnessed them grow professionally. I have watched them face the great challenge of becoming scholars and investigators as they acquired new teaching knowledge and insights. It is through their academic eyes and results that I have seen their professional growth. Indeed, I feel I have actually heard the clicks accompanying their growth.

It is their voices as teacher-inquirers that I sought to portray in this book. Through their research experiences as teacher-inquirers I have come to cherish self-study as a meaningful tool in the hands of the teacher. Hence, I have interwoven their voices into the rich descriptions of their studies. This book would not have been possible without their diligent, systematic, and attentive inquiries. Moreover, this book would not have been possible without their consent to share their studies with the world.

I admire their courage in exposing their work, for self-study by its very nature is personal. Without courage there would never have been any teacher research. Without courage other teachers and educators would not be able to learn about the power of self-study and its impact on teachers' professional identity and growth.

For all this, I thank you: Idit Friedman, who knew right from the start that she would investigate her own story of becoming a teacher "in spite of and regardless of everything "; Galit Attal, who was intrigued by her early kibbutz upbringing and its impact on her adult life as a mother and educator; Mali Yizhak, who was willing to embark on an action research study in order to reveal the true relationship between herself and her instructor colleague; and Hagit Uzan and Michal Vertheimer, who methodically analyzed their authentic instructional situation and creatively proposed another expected instructional situation based on their new knowledge and insights. I also thank my other students who granted their permission to use their instructional situation case analyses (B and C), but wished to remain anonymous. Thank you all for your willingness to share your research data with me and with others. You are true scholar practitioners. Finally, I thank Donna Bossin for her contribution. A special gratitude is given to Levinsky College of Education for its financial support in the production of this book.

CHAPTER 1

INTRODUCTION

This book focuses on self-study and its role in the professional development of teachers. Three methodological approaches are used to describe the nature of self-study and its significance to teachers' professional lives: instructional situations case analysis, critical autobiography and action research. Self-study is presented as a form of research that enables teachers to systematically and rationally examine their professional practice in teaching. Teacher-inquirers pursue self-inquiry by analyzing and processing their instructional situations, i.e., their teaching cases, or by reflectively examining critical events throughout their personal and professional lives. The cases examined by teacher-inquirers are an integral part of their professional experience and represent diverse domains of professional interest, including their work with their pupils in the classroom, interactions with parents, relations with colleagues in the teachers' room, relations with the school principal, supervision of student teachers in their classrooms and other areas as well.

My experience as an instructor and advisor to numerous student teachers pursuing self-studies has led me to believe that every teacher has a case story or a professional life story to tell. Each such story or case is worthy of documentation and analysis and can offer its own insights. Such a case story is only one anecdote in a chain of events that have occurred and will continue to occur to teachers during their teaching career. All three of the approaches outlined above have been examined by students in my graduate level classes. These students are all experienced teachers who went back to school to obtain their M.Ed. degrees. Over the years I have come to value self-study as an important and significant tool in the hands of experienced teachers who, by using these approaches, have successfully integrated theory and practice. All the examples are therefore taken from the self-studies of these students.

The teachers whose instructional situations or cases are described in this book also all happen to be women. At the time, these teachers apparently believed these cases were important and meaningful and therefore chose to write them up so they could learn from them and restructure their practice. Each case described in the chapter on instructional situation analysis, for example, is likely only one of many. The chain of cases in a teacher's professional life is what ultimately comprises the teacher's professional autobiography, as in that described, for example, in the chapter on critical autobiography.

With the exception of the example on action research, all the cases in this book were drawn from memory and are not word-for-word documentation of events in real time. The action research example documents events in real time due to its nature as an action design whose goal is to improve the work of the educator in-action.

Chapter 2 sets the theoretical background for this book. It first describes the current status of research in education in general, and then discusses self-study as a particular research genre. The chapter concludes by examining teacher identity and its relation to self-study as well as considering the role of discourse analysis in revealing a teacher's sense of professional self.

Chapters 3, 4, and 5 express the voices of the teacher-inquirers. Chapter 3 describes the instructional situations case analysis approach, outlines the steps for implementing such analysis and offers three cases written and analyzed by teachers. Instructional situation A comprises the authentic and expected stories written by Hagit Uzan and Michal Vertheimer to describe a case they encountered. Instructional situations B and C represent cases provided by teachers who wished to remain anonymous.

The instructional situations case analysis approach is considered a basic research methodology. In my view, case analysis serves as a first step for teacher practitioners, who are also novice teacher-inquirers, toward more profound understanding and meaningful insight with respect to their teaching practice. Indeed, the approach provides them a means for reconstructing and restructuring their work.

The basic inquiry skills required of a teacher-inquirer include the ability to methodically examine each case, to derive its major themes and to relate these themes to theoretical perspectives. The instructional situations approach was developed during a college course called Instructional Situations Analysis as part of a graduate program on Learning and Instruction.[2]

Chapter 4 describes the critical autobiography approach and exemplifies it with two critical autobiographies originally written by Idit Friedman and Galit Attal. While critical autobiography can also encompass a collection of teaching cases, it is unique in its focus on the teacher's broad professional narrative over time. Critically examining the professional life of the teacher-inquirer and relating the events of this professional life to theoretical considerations can transform this examination into a form of critical research. In this form of autobiography, the teacher-inquirer clarifies and interprets the critical events of life, at the time of analysis as well as within the sociopolitical context in which they occurred, based upon personal and professional insights and knowledge.

Chapter 5 focuses on action research and provides an example of a study conducted by a teacher-instructor. In general, action research is built upon a case or cases of teaching, and can make use of inquiry skills acquired while analyzing the instructional situations. The design of this research can make use of any research paradigm. That is, action research can be based upon a qualitative research paradigm, a quantitative research paradigm, or a paradigm combining the two. In addition to being a form of self-study, action research takes advantage of the cyclical nature of this type of research: investigative examination, generation of new research questions, structuring a plan of action, further investigative examination, and so forth. In this book, action research is exemplified by Mali Yizhak's study. Because so much has already been written on action research in the classroom environment, I chose to use one study only to exemplify this approach. This is a somewhat different "story" of self-study conducted by a teacher-instructor who examined the relationship between herself and her instructor colleague with the aim of improving an integrative school program.

At the end of each chapter, the teacher's identity is further examined through discourse analysis to reveal the teacher-inquirer's sense of professional self. Through critical discourse analysis, I as an external researcher can expose a teacher's professional identity and thus illustrate how self-study contributes to the evolving professional self of that particular teacher. At the same time, such analysis can show how a teacher's identity can change, depending on the context in which the study was implemented. Even when teachers report on research that provided them with new insights and generated new knowledge, they still are unable to recognize their professional identity. This is where critical discourse analysis steps in. It enables us, researchers and educators, to become acquainted with the teacher-inquirers involved in a self-study. It also enables us to understand their sense of professional self in a given situation and helps us realize how this sense of self might change under different circumstances. For teachers, in effect, their newly understood sense of professional self complements the additional knowledge and insights they derive from their study. Indeed, the very act of self-study is what enables teacher-inquirers to gather new knowledge and gain in-depth insights that pave their way to new practices. On the other hand, discourse analysis is analogous to putting a mirror in front of the teachers by letting them and the entire educational world know about their sense of professional self. This newly acquired knowledge and self-awareness complete the picture of teacher-inquirers as scholarly practitioners. I believe that self-study enables teachers to assume their own true identity as teachers. Discourse analysis of their narratives helps reveal what lies beneath the surface for every teacher: a well-defined sense of professional self.

The concluding chapter ties the three approaches together and discusses some of the main points discussed in the previous chapters.

The three approaches presented in this book share a number of attributes. All focus on the professional practice of teacher-inquirers, all interpret situations from the teacher-inquirer's perspective, all provide systematic investigative methods directed toward the professional development of the teacher-inquirer, and all involve structuring new courses of action based on research insights.

The different approaches to self-study described in this book were developed based upon the scholarship of teaching. According to this perspective, the academic involvement of teachers in their own teaching forms the foundation for their professional development over time (Zeichner, 1999). It has always been the case that the most obvious source from which teachers can learn is other teachers. Today, many voices among researchers and educators claim that in practice teachers are the most important decision-makers in education systems, and they should make such decisions consciously and deliberately, based upon their own practice (McLaughlin, Black-Hawkins, McIntyre, & Townsend, 2008). Therefore, a self-study approach may be a powerful tool in refining the practice of teaching.

The instructional situations approach, for example, derives its essence in part from the case analysis perspective in teaching, introduced in Israel by Silberstein (2002) in his book *Mentoring and Teaching Events: Pedagogy of Case Literature in Teacher Education*. In the two chapters I wrote for the Silberstein book, I focused on case-based work in teaching, and for the most part on cases of others analyzed by an outside researcher (see Ezer, 2002a, 2002b). The current book, in contrast, shows how teacher-inquirers themselves develop a case-based research approach. The analyses are retrospective rather than from the immediate perspective of the teaching event. Moreover, the approach put forward in the book involves developing interpretive strategies and processing future insights based upon interpretation.

The self-study approaches discussed in this book are intended to reinforce teachers' perception of themselves as "teacher-inquirers" throughout their professional lives. Furthermore, they reflect the notion that research is crucial to professional development in that it provides teacher-inquirers a meaningful tool that can be implemented in the teaching space between theory and practice. It also provides other teachers and educators an emic and rich view of the teaching profession and brings to light the transformative perspective of teacher-inquirers based on their self-studies. I began by saying that teachers learn from the experiences of other teachers. I will end by saying that teachers also learn from their own self-studied experiences.

RESEARCH IN EDUCATION, SELF-STUDY AND TEACHER IDENTITY

This chapter provides a current perspective on research in education in general and considers how self-study evolved as an independent research genre. First, I establish the position of research within the educational context. Next, I examine self-study as a research genre within the context of practitioner research and scholarship of teaching. Finally, I discuss the accumulated body of knowledge describing teacher identity and the role of discourse analysis in revealing a teacher's sense of professional self.

EDUCATIONAL RESEARCH

In educational research today, diverse research genres have become the focus of much research attention (Kennedy, 2005). Research genres vary greatly. At one end of the spectrum are positive (objective) and primarily post-positive studies that take a broad view of the educational system, teacher education institutes and teacher education in general. At the other end is qualitative research covering numerous research traditions, such as biography/narrative studies, ethnography, case studies, grounded theory, phenomenological study and combinations of all of these (Creswell, 1998; Sabar Ben-Yehoshua, 2001). This type of research is marked by a profound understanding of the subject under investigation using research tools such as interviews, observations and document analysis (Sabar Ben-Yehoshua, 1990; Shkedi, 2004). Creswell (1998) views qualitative research as the process of examining understanding, based on distinct investigative methodologies that expose social or human problems. The researcher constructs a complex, holistic picture, analyzes words, reports the detailed points of view of the research subjects and carries out the research in a natural environment. Mixed method research, marked by the integration of quantitative and qualitative methods, has also gained considerable standing in the design of educational research studies (Bryman, 2006; Onwuegbuzie, Withcer, Collins, Filer, Wiedmaier, & Moore, 2007; Tashakkori & Teddlie, 2008).

The range of research studies available to educational researchers is particularly extensive. Within the context of research genres in education, there are those who advocate experimental studies and those who support the numerous qualitative research traditions. Because teachers are at the center of professional achievement in the educational system, they are expected to have more authoritative knowledge (for example, in experimental studies), more dynamic knowledge about educational figures who expose different truths (in narrative studies, for instance, when teachers get a chance to share contrasting stories) or more detailed knowledge (as in that emerging from ethnographic research) (Kennedy, 1999). Whatever the case, it seems that research is guided by the perspectives or beliefs of the researchers and by "paradigms of research that are imitated within any given field" (Tashakkori & Teddlie, 2008, p. 8). Tashakkori and Teddlie define paradigms as "the worldviews or belief systems that guide researchers" (p. 7). The positivist paradigm provides the basis for quantitative methods, while qualitative methods are based upon the constructivist paradigm (Tashakkori & Teddlie, 2008).

Borko, Whitcomb, and Byrnes (2008) discuss four research genres in teacher education: a) The genre known "effects of teacher education" research refers to a body of scholarship concerned with understanding the relationships between teacher education experiences and student learning. Its roots can be found in the scientific method of the natural sciences; b) "Interpretive research" is a search for local meanings and encompasses research traditions such as ethnography, narrative, phenomenology, and discourse analysis; c) "Practitioner research" of those who "actually do the work of teacher education" (p.1029) includes action research, participatory research, self-study, and teacher research; d) "Design research" involves a systematic design and study of instructional strategies and tools, characterized by an intimate relationship between the improvement of practice and the development of theory.

The struggle over research methods is potentially healthy. Yet according to researchers such as Kennedy (2005), when it comes to "the paradigm wars" this struggle leaves something to be desired. It compels dichotomous thinking according to which one side or the other must be in control, without leaving room for healthy dispute. Those who advocate a clear separation between the two paradigms base their thinking on the incompatibility thesis, according to which researchers who integrate the two paradigms in their work are doomed to failure due to the inherent philosophical differences between the two (Tashakkori & Teddlie, 2008). According to Kennedy (2005), the view that researchers must engage in rigorous research was prevalent from the 1940s through the 1960s, a period marked by the use of statistical methods in complex experimental research. The need to be in control was one of the reasons that researchers felt they must carry out their research under laboratory conditions. The 1960s and 1970s saw a shift to field studies and quasi-experimental research (Borko et al., 2008). This type of research began to run into complications due to the problem of defining the effects in the field of the various parties involved (i.e. principals, teachers, parents). Although field studies were clearly important, it soon became apparent that they were difficult to carry out. Concurrently, researchers began to realize that educational events are not controlled by universal laws of cause and effect but rather by the individual intentions of those participating in the event and by the simultaneous effects of interactions. Moreover, it gradually became evident that significance would emerge only in context, thus necessitating detailed and prolific descriptions. These concepts gained momentum in case studies and ethnographic studies of the 1980s. Today many consider narrative analysis to be the preferred research genre in education (Kennedy, 2005). This view is in line with postmodern claims with respect to the structuring of culture and multiculturalism and the relative nature of knowledge.

Theoreticians such as Tashakkori and Teddlie (2008) and Denzin (2008) advocate pragmatism and the compatibility thesis, according to which the two paradigms, the qualitative and the quantitative, can complement each other by means of different combinations. In fact, Denzin (2008), following Teddlie and Tashakkori (2003), talks about "the third moment" and the new paradigm dialogs to describe an epistemological position that evolved out the discussions and controversies associated with the 1980's paradigm wars. "The third moment mediates quantitative and qualitative disputes by finding a third, or middle ground" (p. 317), he claims. In this context, Hostetler (2005) has proposed the multimethods approach, which is meant to provide data useful to theoreticians and participants as well. Nevertheless, Hostetler believes that good research is not only a matter of adequate processes. It also involves objectives and results that contribute to the different participants, a view that naturally supports applied research in education. Borko et al. (2008) recommend integrating different research genres in accordance with the research question and for the sake of promoting achievements in education based upon research evidence.

Research in the field of education is embroiled in another struggle as well—the struggle for its own legitimacy. Indeed, Loewenberg-Ball and Forzani (2007) maintain that there are those who actually denounce educational research by claiming it is ineffective and demands limited intellectual requirements of its researchers. Those who denounce research in education also assert that educational researchers in teacher education and in the school system are not on a very high level. Evans (2002) sees this as an attack on educational research and claims that it is important to address the issue of criticism of educational research.

Nevertheless, a large and extensive group of researchers acknowledge the quality of educational research, refer to the need for applied research in the educational field, and encourage teachers to investigate their own work as part of their professional development (Burkhardt & Schoenfeld, 2003). Supporters of research in the field of education argue that research and politics go hand in hand (Cohen, Manion, & Morrison, 2007). They claim that educational research is essential to create a form of disciplined knowledge that can contribute directly to solving the pressing problems in education, both among those participating in teaching practice, i.e. the teachers, and among those who set the policies and make the decisions (Loewenberg Ball & Forzani, 2007). Furthermore, Loewenberg Ball and Forzani (2007) maintain that the central goal of teacher training must be to develop a professional teacher-education program focusing on research with the goal of training the next generation of academics who are themselves researchers. Such training must help beginning education researchers to a) understand the environments and problems that are the focus of education research; b) develop questions for study that are central to education ; c) learn to design and choose appropriate methods for education research. In this sense, research becomes a practical work tool for teachers and an integral part of their practice as teachers. Teachers are seen as central figures in the educational research arena for they are part of the reciprocal teacher-pupil-school relationship.

Based on the above, multiple interpretations of the same event are considered significant in educational research today. Kincheloe and Tobin (2006), for example, maintain that different observers will have different interpretations of the same event. Diverse values, ideologies and positions will lead individuals to interpret events differently. Researchers today understand that those who generate the knowledge—teachers and students— perceive the world from their individual perspectives. They position themselves in the center and are shaped by the cultural and social context in which they operate. Moreover, researchers frame their research in a language that encompasses the teacher-inquirers' latent perceptions. Therefore, teacher research is frequently advocated as a form of professional development, a way for teachers to learn to examine their own contexts and their own practices more critically (Kennedy, 1999). This kind of research is, in fact, an integral part of the new professionalism that has emerged as a recognized feature of the teaching profession (Evans, 2002).

Over the past two decades, then, teacher education has begun to shift its attention toward a systematic examination of teachers' professional experiences. This shift reflects a clear understanding that nurturing teachers as inquirers will help schools develop and improve, based on the assumption that it is the teacher who makes decisions in the classroom. Hence, teachers are seen as researchers (Zeichner & Conklin, 2005) who can collect data on their work by means of diaries, video recordings, autobiographical writings and other research formats.

SELF-STUDY, THE TEACHER-INQUIRER AND PROFESSIONAL IDENTITY

Self-study takes its place among existing research genres and within the interpretive view of educational research as an applied research approach available to practitioners, who in our case are educators as well. In this type of research, the development of the "self" is examined within the teaching context, under the assumption that professionals are examining themselves (Bullough & Pinnegar, 2004). This type of research can be quantitative, qualitative, or a combination of both. Indeed, in this type of research as well, a "war" is being waged. Bullough and Pinnegar (2004) identify one of the difficulties in education research as the struggle between the educational disciplines involved in teacher training on the one hand and the teacher educators and teachers themselves on the other. Psychologists, for example, have been claiming for some time now that research on teaching and learning is their territory. In contrast, Bullough and Pinnegar (2004) maintain that the history of teaching and learning research has shown that when researchers began to investigate how teachers understand knowledge, they inevitably began respecting teachers more. For them to understand how beliefs and knowledge were related to practice, they had to get closer to the teachers. As a result, new practices in teacher education developed, paving the way for teachers to investigate their own work.

Therefore, the higher education system has recently become more open to self-study in the colleges and universities, particularly within the teacher education community. Self-study is not homogeneous in nature, and is characterized by a number of traditions or trends. It comprises, for example, action research and critical autobiography, as well as basic tools for self-inquiry in professional practice, such as reflection, an essential skill in self-study. Critical autobiography demands superior investigative skills and more complex research tools compared to those used in reflection. These tools can include interviews and even questionnaires.

The analysis of instructional situations or cases also is a form of self-study especially appropriate to the professional atmosphere in education. This is a basic and initial means available to teacher-inquirers. It enables them to acquire methical tools for systematic observation of the teaching cases in which they are involved. These tools can also be applied to other forms of self-study they wish to undertake in their professional workspace. As mentioned, many of these basic skills involve reflection, but also participatory observation capabilities and interpretation based upon the theoretical literature, as outlined in the next section.

In the following section, I review the developments in self-study research in education and teacher education and then discuss the relation between this research and the development of a professional identity. At the end of the chapter I also discuss the role of meta-analysis in examining teacher research for the purpose of revealing a teacher's sense of professional self.

Self-Study in Teacher Education

Zeichner (1999) perceives self-study as "research about teacher education [that] is being conducted by those who actually do the work of teacher education" (p. 8). He claims that "the birth of the self study in teacher education movement around 1990 has been probably the single most significant development ever in the field of teacher education research" (p. 8). In fact, instead of research *on* teaching and teacher education by an outside party, it is research by teachers and teacher educators *about* their practice (Borko et al., 2008).

In general, what makes self-study unique in education is that it enables the voices of teachers to be heard and helps nurture their professional development in its working space between theory and practice (Bullough & Pinnegar, 2001; 2004). Self-study is situated within the genre of practitioner research (Borko et al., 2008), and sometimes referred to as teacher research, or reflective practice (Evans, 2002).

Cole and Knowles (2000) broaden the emphasis in teacher inquiry, claiming that "teaching is researching" (p. 1). That is, they see theory as embedded in practice rather than as a way to implement practice. In their view, teachers develop over a continuum that begins long before they undertake any formal teacher training programs and continues throughout their formal education and their first years of teaching up through their retirement, at which time they have gained rich and abundant experience. Cole and Knowles (2000) believe that by means of systematic reflection and analysis of practice, teachers become responsible for their own professional development. They refer to this process as *reflexive inquiry*, indicating that a teacher's teaching and development "are rooted in the 'personal'" (p. 2). That is, teaching reflects teachers as individuals, their values and beliefs, their perspectives and experiences as they develop throughout their lives. These researchers believe that for teachers to understand their professional lives and work and develop professionally, they must understand the formative stage as well as their ongoing experiences and the influences shaping their perspectives and practices.

In addition to the notion of reflexive inquiry, Cole and Knowles also introduce the concept of *reflective inquiry*. This concept involves an ongoing process of examining and refining practice by focusing on various work contexts: personal, pedagogical, curricular, intellectual, social and ethical. All this is based upon the notion that the assumptions of practice are subject to ongoing questioning. According to Kubler LaBoskey (2005), reflection is a personal process of thinking, refining, redefining and developing actions that continues throughout self-study. In fact, reflection requires directed, conscious and intentional thinking about past actions with a view toward future improvement and progress (Margolin, Ezer, & Silberstein, 2001; Silberstein, 1998). Reflection, in essence, involves "looking backwards" or "projecting one's vision backward onto an action, an event or an incident" (Silberstein, 1998, p. 16). Nevertheless, even if necessary for self-study, this process is not sufficient for undertaking the research.

In contrast, Cole and Knowles (2000) believe that *reflexive inquiry* is "reflective inquiry situated within the context of personal histories in order to make connections between personal lives and professional careers, and to understand personal (including early) influences on professional practice" (p. 2). In other words, *reflexive inquiry* takes into account personal history that is based upon contextual elements of understanding. It stresses the basic role of experience in shaping practice in a way that *reflective inquiry* cannot do. *Reflexive inquiry* is based upon a critical perspective that encompasses examining the status quo and norms of practice, particularly with respect to issues of power and control. *Reflexive inquiry* can also be understood through a metaphor of mirrors and prisms. Being reflexive is like seeing practice through mirrors and transparent prisms in which the various components are refracted, perhaps enlarged or broken down into the different colors of the spectrum. *Reflexive inquiry* considers different elements throughout life, in school and out, and examines their colors, features and implications for professional life. Another feature of *reflexive inquiry* is "that, unlike traditional research, it is not a linear, sequential process; it is more spiral or cyclical. Thus the research process requires ongoing reflection, analysis, and responsiveness" (Cole & Knowles, 2000, p. 104).

Bullough and Pinnegar (2004) claim that self-study and reflective practice are not one and the same, for reflection is always embedded within the individual, while self-study derives from communication with others and is in essence for the sake of others and together with others. Nonetheless, they agree that the "self" is understood as reflective with respect to the individual, institution or plan examining itself in-action with the goal of examining the relation between belief (or knowledge) and practice. It is these ideas that define the "self." Hence, self-study is used for teaching and examining experience in order to better understand the "self," that is, teaching, learning and developing related knowledge. Indeed, we can say that reflection is one of the tools at the disposal of self-inquirers, but it is not the only one. Teacher-inquirers can use a variety of tools to carry out their self-study, from the quantitative as well as the qualitative paradigm.

Self-study in teacher education is part of the transformation in teacher training research during the last quarter of the 20th century (Bullough & Pinnegar, 2001; Loughran, 2007). It has also become more and more common in other disciplines, among them anthropology, linguistics and economics. According to Bullough and Pinnegar (2001), self-study developed out of and was influenced by at least four different fields of research in education. The first is the emergence of naturalistic and qualitative research and the redefinition of validity and accuracy. Despite the controversies surrounding this matter, a new understanding of the relations between researcher and subject has emerged. There are those who claim that researchers no longer have at their disposal objects that are external to the research and to time, whether expected or static (i.e., unable to be changed). Many researchers have now accepted the fact that they are highly involved in their own research, even personally. The stage was set fifty years ago by Ross Mooney, who discussed the personal nature of research. Mooney's perception is quoted by Ketelle (2004, pp. 452–453):

> ...a personal venture which, quite aside from its social benefits, is worth doing for its direct contribution to one's own self-realization. It can be taken as a way of meeting life with maximum of stops open to get out of the experience its most poignant significance, its most full-throated song (Mooney, 1957, p. 155).

Hence, the identity of the researcher is central to research work.

The second inspiration for self-study, according to Bullough and Pinnegar (2001), came from the reconceptualist movement in curriculum studies. This approach is based upon the belief that one always teaches the self. A teacher is described as someone setting out on a quest to seek the roots of self-understanding in order to nurture that understanding in education. Even though this approach has been embroiled in controversy, the movement attracted a generation of young people, now middle-aged academics, that helped make self-study a central practice in education.

The third factor that has served to promote self-study is related to the growing involvement of researchers worldwide in teacher training. These researchers bring along with them diverse intellectual traditions based in the humanities and not necessarily in the social sciences. Van Manen (1980), for example, raised interest in phenomenology and the nature of experience that had developed in Holland. Similarly, Clandinin and Connelly (2000) heightened awareness of the narrative nature of knowing and the place of stories in teachers' development and understanding of practice.

Action research constitutes the fourth influential factor on self-study. Cochran-Smith and Lytle (1993) developed models for investigating teachers that make it possible to preserve researcher/practitioner distinctions. All research in this field requires redefining the roles and relationships of the practitioner.

As mentioned, self-study is a form of inquiry in which teachers examine their beliefs and actions in the context of their work as educators for the purpose of raising pedagogical questions (Whitehead, 1993). The objective of those engaged in self-study in education is to understand teaching from the inside out rather than from the outside in, and at the same time to implement in practice what was discovered from the research (Bullough & Pinnegar, 2004). Self-study offers a methodology appropriate for improving the quality of teacher training and for creating knowledge about teaching and learning.

According to Bullough and Pinnegar (2004) the definition of self-study is hard to pin down, and is considered anew each time researchers in the field gather together. Yet those engaged in this field share the common assumption that self-study involves recognizing that teachers are caught between two worlds: that of practice and that of scientific research in education. This assumption is based upon the notion that our knowledge about teaching/learning derives from contextual information created by the knower in a particular situation (Bass, Anderson-Patton, & Allender, 2002). This field of research challenges teacher-educators to adopt a powerful research tool as an integral part of their professional work context to serve a number of objectives in teaching and in teacher training programs (Dinkelman, 2003; Mitchell & Weber, 2005; Mueller, 2003). In so doing, teachers are able to learn from their own experience as well as explain their investigation of their practice more accurately. Dinkelman (2003) asserts that self-study in teacher training is both a means and an end in the advancement of the teaching profession. When teacher educators adopt the concept of self-study as an integral part of their practice, the course of teacher training is likely to undergo change. In effect, as Bullough and Pinnegar (2001) claim, the researcher engaged in self-study stands at the crossroads between biography and history. The questions posed by this researcher emerge from the interaction between the self as an educator, in context and over time, and others who are committed to nurturing young learners, as well as from the impact of this interaction on the self and on others. In their view, "ultimately, the aim of self-study research is moral, to gain understanding necessary to make that interaction increasingly educative" (Bullough & Pinnegar, 2001, p. 15).

Berry (2004) reviews four leading reasons for teacher educators to engage in self-study: 1) the need to examine the degree of congruence and consistency between their beliefs and their practice; 2) the need to study a particular aspect of teaching practice in-depth; 3) the desire to develop a model of critical reflection with respect to teachers' work; 4) the desire to create meaningful alternatives for institutional evaluation.

What, then, makes self-study worth reading or deserving of the title "research"? Bullough and Pinnegar (2001) attempt to answer this question by setting criteria for determining research quality. Because teachers engaged in self-study often examine their own biographies, Bullough and Pinnegar claim that the teacher-inquirer's history and personal biography must be balanced against the broader context in which he or she operates. This balance should be expressed not only in the data gathered (from self and others) and written up, but also in the methods used to analyze the data and to present the results orally and in writing. These researchers believe the following:

> . . . although the final story of being or becoming a teacher educator never will be told, . . . more powerful narrative self-studies will follow careful attention to the guidelines we have identified: A self-study is a good read, attends to the "nodal moments" of teaching and being a teacher educator and thereby enables reader insight or understanding into self, reveals a lively conscience and balanced sense of self-importance, tells a recognizable teacher or teacher educator story, portrays character development in the face of serious issues within a complex setting, gives place to the dynamic struggle of living life whole, and offers new perspective (Bullough & Pinnegar, 2001, p. 19).

Further, according to Bullough and Pinnegar (2001), the self-study researcher must edit the text, yet must not offer interpretations that are contradictory to the data. This is a matter of conscience, credibility and sincerity, obliging the researcher to view the data properly and without distortions. The second issue is that the text must be interesting at the very least, if not provocative. Hence there is value in the alternative perspectives offered by the teacher-inquirer. Bullough and Pinnegar (2004) note that self-study, like any good form of research, must be systematic, make use of sufficient, stable and empirical data, and be totally transparent.

Self-study research is not destined to remain the sole property of the researcher. Therefore it must be considered not only within the context of clarification and reflection as stable and meaningful work tools for teachers, but also as a means of nurturing communities of learning and inquiring teachers. Self-study offers many such opportunities. Therefore it can enlighten the practice both of schoolteachers and of teacher-educators and can enrich the knowledge of members of both these groups. As teacher-educators discuss issues of teacher training, learning and self-study more and more, the community of learners among teacher-educators will grow, leading to significant changes in the field of teacher education.

Russell (2006) notes that self-study research relies upon the interaction between close colleagues actively and constructively listening to one another. Indeed, the ideas and interpretations emerging from the teaching experience of professional educators, when systematically presented and based upon findings, create a reflective community and promote change in the broad field of teacher education. Goodnough (2005) emphasizes that self-study, whether individual or cooperative, is extremely valuable in improving individual practice. At the same time, it has the potential to advance other fields of interest such as the science of education, by developing abundant professional knowledge based upon teaching/learning.

One of the problems in self-study revolves around the relation between the "self" researcher and the research subjects. Zellermayer and Keiny (2006), for example, refer to action research and note that in qualitative research this matter is considered an ethical issue, raising numerous questions: What is the place of the "self" in action research? What is the relationship between the researcher and the research subjects? What research methodology can be derived from this? Can action research refer to an individual, whether researcher or research subject? How can the researcher's reflections on the processes he or she is undergoing be integrated into the research description? How can other participants as well as the readers be included? Finally, how can a reciprocal relationship be created between the data collected by the researcher and those gathered by the other participants? In fact, the growing numbers of teachers involved in self-studies in schools are less formally grounded either in research methods or in ethical safeguards (Zeni, 2001). Zellermayer and Keiny

(2006) claim these questions have motivated some researchers to attempt to construct professional research/learning communities in the organizations where they work. These researchers seek to examine their role and status through self-study and their individual ability to construct a research community. At the same time they must try to define a research space for themselves that will not hinder their efforts to build the community but rather support this work. In this way the role of the "self" in individual action research can be determined, whether the individual is the researcher or the research subject. Indeed, the individual can be seen as part of the human-social setting: the self as part of the community, the self as part of the interpersonal discourse, and the post-modern perception of the self developing the individual's unique nature, personal freedom and freedom of choice.

Feldman (2003) raises the question of how researchers can know they have actually changed their ways and how they can convince others not only that a change has taken place but also that this change is beneficial and substantive. This is one of the reasons why self-study researchers prefer to use such research methodologies as autobiographical research and narrative research. These investigators not only seek to examine educational practices. They also seek to improve them, based upon their critical autobiography or narrative research, in a particular way that will have an impact on what is happening in the teacher education colleges, universities and schools. Consequently, self-study raises the question of ethical responsibility not only in evaluating the merit or quality of the research but also in assessing its validity. Indeed, the practical applications for teachers' work are the most important and meaningful. Self-study incorporates the pragmatic component in the personal work of every teacher and educator. Hence, it must be solidly grounded, sound and able to provide the required results. In order to increase the validity of self-study, researchers should make validity their essential focus by openly explaining their understanding of the research. This can be accomplished in a number of ways. One is by providing a clear and detailed description of the data collection method and by explicitly clarifying the data source, either within the text or as an appendix. Researchers should also provide details about their research methods, supply evidence of the value of changes in teaching and training methods, suggest creative ways of understanding the raw data and turning it into findings, and expand the triangulation beyond the data sources to include diverse methods in their studies. These steps and others as well can help researchers convince their readers of the validity of their research. In fact, there will be those who define self-study as ethical and political activity (Feldman, 2003; Zeni, 2001). Whether it is called self-study, action research, teacher research or practitioner research, this approach confronts ethical dilemmas and requires systematic and rigorous research methodology. If this type of research ultimately is to produce results and generate change in how researchers conduct themselves as teachers, educators, and teacher-educators, there must be evidence of its value. The research report, in addition to outlining the research focus, importance and method, must also show what was discovered in "seeing beyond the self" and how the research was developed and implemented. Hence, the research must be presented from a number of perspectives (Loughran, 2007).

Self-study, then, is conducted by means of a systematic methodology. There is no single or most correct way to carry out the research. What is important and meaningful is that the study be carried out in a systematic fashion, including collecting data from a number of sources, analyzing them methodically and reporting on them in a way that others can learn from them in order to develop knowledge regarding practice in education (Loughran, 2007; Pinnegar, 1998).

Scholarship of Teaching

Self-study using case literature or instructional situations analysis developed within a broader approach that stresses the importance of the teacher's academic knowledge, as derived from investigating the teacher's work and from the work itself as part of the teacher's professional development. This approach to researching teacher education throughout the teacher's professional life is known as the scholarship of teaching (Hutchings & Shulman, 1999). This approach considers the teacher-inquirer who examines his or her own teaching processes through a series of self-studies, including action research (Zeichner, 2005). The scholarship of teaching is based upon the assumption that the teacher must take an active role in creating knowledge, and not only in processing and transmitting knowledge (Cole & Knowles, 2000). This active role requires meta-skills, that is, observing and examining the very act of teaching. For example, collecting case stories can involve different types of cases, among them narratives, vignettes, episodes and autobiographies. These genres call for different types of research, such as narrative research, action research and self-study in the form of critical autobiography. External investigators collecting cases about teachers will likely use narrative research or qualitative grounded theory research. Teachers, on the other hand, in collecting their own cases and analyzing them critically, will use critical autobiography or reflective analysis of instructional cases. This can be part of the teacher's action research if it continues over time and produces insights regarding the teacher's work. All

17

of these methods that examine the thinking, teaching and practical knowledge of teachers point to the value of narratives, stories and cases in putting forth what teachers know (Hashweh, 2004; Lyons & Kubler LaBoskey, 2005).

Over the past two decades, the emphasis in teacher education seems to have shifted from science, with its focus on rules, variables and proofs, to literature, in which events and narratives play a prominent role. The role of the story or narrative in teacher education developed in the early 1990s and quickly gained momentum. A story is essentially composed of incidents, characters and context, and is organized around a sequence of events occurring at a particular time and place. It offers information about how things work, and its incidents are meaningful. A story is interesting, alive and authentic, and it enables the voices of the narrator and the characters to be heard. Cases in the form of stories also suggest meanings that cannot be gleaned otherwise (Carter, 1999). According to Carter (1999), stories are at the center of teachers' lives. They provide a way to capture the wealth of a particular event or experience, a means of knowing, thinking and reaching a rich understanding of practice. Indeed, this is the knowledge emerging from the very act of teaching. Carter stresses that to know teaching is to know its stories. Stories are the knowledge base in teaching and the core of the teacher training curriculum. These stories also have a narrative whose meaning differs slightly from that of an ordinary story. This approach refers to biography and autobiography, and emphasizes the notion that we live "narrative lives."

Clandinin and Connelly (2000) have worked with teachers over time, observing lessons, writing diaries, holding discussions, documenting and structuring stories, all in order to understand how teachers create meaning from their practice. They focus on narrative research, which is common today in teacher education and is usually carried out by external researchers. In such cases, the teachers are the research object, and their stories are the raw material from which external researchers learn about the teaching act. On the other hand, when teachers use narrative self-studies, their case stories and critical autobiographies constitute raw material for the teachers themselves. They can use this raw material to learn about their own practice and to reach new insights they ordinarily would not be able to attain in the hectic daily routine of their work. Some consider narrative self-study as a way of life for teachers (Kubler LaBoskey, 2005), particularly by means of critical reflection on their work.

In conclusion, self-study in the field of teacher education is only in its infancy. Its continuation as a movement is dependent upon the reliability and significance of its findings. Self-study critically examines the themes arising from the data and attempts to answer the questions "so what." Self-study seeks to arouse, challenge and enlighten, though not necessarily explain what is already known. In the form of autobiography or documenting and analyzing instructional situations, self-study confronts the writer with special requirements. The text must be readable, proven, and transparent (for example, the relationship between autobiography and history). The issues must be central to the field of education, and sufficient information should be provided so the reader can acknowledge the text's academic authority, not just its authenticity (Bullough & Pinnegar, 2001).

Self-study is carried out by the researcher, who also writes the research reports. These results are usually narratives that can be used to reveal the teacher-inquirer's professional identity by means of critical discourse analysis. In the following section, I therefore discuss the notion of a teacher's professional identity, or sense of professional self. I also elaborate on discourse analysis as a tool for revealing attributes related to the professional identity of the teacher who has written the research report.

TEACHERS' PROFESSIONAL IDENTITY

Over the past twenty years, many researchers have considered the issue of teacher identity. Nias (1989) was one of the first to examine the complex identities of teachers constructed in and through discourse. These various identities swirl around teacher education programs, schools and the classroom environment, as well as around teachers' personal lives. Nias (1989) breaks down the term "teachers' professional identity" into two definitions. One is a freer and looser definition of a teacher's professional "sense of self" and identity, while the other refers to a teacher's fixed, unchanging and stable "substantive self." By working with notions of multiple professional identities, a teacher can work in different contexts and with different people and accommodate to various interpretations of the teaching profession (Bloom & Munro, 1995). In general, theorists today have called upon teachers to become aware of their identities and the political, historical, and social forces shaping these identities. Yet it still remains unclear how the concepts of identity and self are exactly related (Rodgers & Scott, 2008).

Rodgers and Scott (2008) claim that contemporary conceptions of identity share four basic assumptions (p. 733): (1) Identity is dependent upon and formed within multiple contexts that bring social, cultural, political, and historical forces into play; (2) Identity is formed in relationships with others and involves emotions; (3) Identity is shifting, unstable, and multiple; (4)

Identity involves the construction and reconstruction of meaning through stories over time.

Following upon Maclure (1993) and Feiman-Nemser (2001), Flores and Day (2006) understand identity as an ongoing and dynamic process that entails making sense of and reinterpreting one's own values and experiences. Becoming a teacher involves, in essence, a transformation of the teacher's identity. This transformation is possible through a process in which "teachers use, justify, explain and make sense of themselves in relation to other people, and to the contexts in which they operate" (Maclure, 1993, p. 312).

Researchers believe it is important to study how teachers perceive themselves, since their identities strongly influence their judgments and behavior (Nias, 1989; Beijaard et al., 2000). The impact of the workplace (positive or negative) and perceptions of school culture and leadership have played a key role in (re)shaping teachers' understanding of teaching, facilitating or hindering their professional development and (re)constructing their professional identities. These researchers believe that a sense of professional identity can contribute to teachers' self-efficacy, motivation, commitment and job satisfaction. This identity is therefore a key factor in their becoming and continuing to be effective teachers in the future. Moreover, teachers should strive to become aware of their own identity and the contexts, relationships, and emotions shaping this identity. Indeed, they should reclaim the authority of their own voice (Rodgers & Scott, 2008).

A study by Beijaard (1995) defines teacher identity on the basis of three distinctive categories: the subject taught by the teacher, the teacher's relationship with the students, and the teacher's role or role conception. For each category, teachers were asked to clarify their actual perceptions and prior knowledge. In a later study, Beijaard, Verloop, and Vermunt (2000) found that teachers' professional identity emerges from how they see themselves as subject matter experts, pedagogical experts, and didactical experts.

Some researchers (e.g., Elbaz-Luwisch, 2005; Goodson, 1992) emphasize the personal dimension in teaching and are particularly interested in how teachers' past personal life experiences interact with their professional lives. This kind of research on teacher biographies and autobiographies focuses on critical incidents and events assumed to shape their professional image. The teachers are given an opportunity to see themselves as learners through incidents at work, together with other dramatic occurrences in their personal lives. Roberts-Holmes (2003) presents a similar perspective by examining how the professional identities of primary teachers in Gambia have been shaped by the hegemonic discourses of Gambian nationalism and

Islam, according to which these teachers are taught to see teaching as a "noble profession." Roberts-Holmes found that their working lives were based upon histories, religions and cultures, and in this context they described their emotional and political commitment to the "noble profession" of teaching. This commitment was based upon the hegemonic discourses of nationalism and Islam.

Doecke (2004) argues that in order to capture the complexities of her work as a teacher-educator and view her identity as a teacher-educator in the college where she works, she must tell another story, a counter narrative that can continually question the beliefs and values at the core of her professional life. This counter narrative helped her realize that her professional identity as a teacher educator puts her at odds with the official curriculum and policy context in which she is obliged to operate. Her study, a self-study, helped her focus on the professional learning she experienced by interacting with her students in the classroom or during school visits. These interactions enabled her to perceive her professional identity as conflicting with existing policy, including managerial attempts to define acceptable educational "outcomes" and other global pressures to adopt a uniform worldview. In other words, she was able to theorize the relationship between her professional practice and the world in which she operates.

Robinson and McMillan (2006) claim that understanding the identities teacher-educators construct for themselves is central to effecting innovation within a changing policy environment. Thus, identity plays a significant role in educational change. They believe that by accessing people's perspectives, values, motivations, attitudes and views prior to implementing change, change agents are able to tap into existing strands of identity, thereby facilitating a weaving together of old and new roles and responsibilities. A teacher-educator's identity is, therefore, most likely to succeed when the values of the "new" identity build directly upon those of the "old" identity.

Since the definition of the self is somewhat elusive, I have chosen to adopt Rodgers and Scott's attitude towards the self. They believe the self subsumes teacher identities and is "an evolving, yet coherent being that consciously and unconsciously constructs and is constructed, reconstructs and is reconstructed in interaction with cultural contexts, institutions, and people with which the self lives, learns, and functions" (Rodgers & Scott, 2008, p. 751). Rodgers and Scott assume that for teachers to become aware of their own selves, they must know themselves and their own frames of reference, values and biases. Teachers should take a critical look at themselves and the privileges and inequities of their own lives and those of their students. Teachers should explore their own social perspectives.

Teachers should reflect upon their educational experiences as children, and recognize how these experiences impact how they think about teaching. Teachers should be exposed to perspectives different from their own.

The studies described in this book offer some relevant insights into the similarities and differences of how teachers perceive their professional identity, including changes in identity and relevant learning experiences throughout their careers. The teacher-inquirers' self-studies are analyzed by me in my capacity as an external investigator, in order to provide some insights into the sense of professional self of these teachers. For this purpose, I use critical discourse analysis to enhance the investigation of teachers' professional identity. I further argue that discourse analysis unveils teachers' hidden, covert sense of professional self. Since critical discourse analysis is a useful tool in revealing professional identity among teachers, I discuss this method in detail in the next section.

Critical Discourse Analysis

Critical discourse analysis focuses on social and political issues related to texts and text production. It also systematically examines the subject matter of discourse and the social relations, assumptions and ideological complexes informing it (Georgakopolou & Goutsos, 1999). In general, critical discourse analysis studies how social power abuse, dominance, and inequality are enacted, reproduced, and resisted by text and talk in the social and political context (Van Dijk, 2001). This interdisciplinary approach to language study adopts a critical point of view in order to study language behavior in natural speech situations of social relevance. It focuses on how social relations, identity, knowledge and power are constructed through written and spoken texts in communities, schools and classrooms (Gee, 1999; Luke, 1994; Van Dijk, 2001).

The terms "discourse" and "discourse analysis" have different meanings to scholars in different fields. Linguists talk about anything beyond the study of language use. Critical theorists and others talk about the "discourse of power" and the "discourse of racism," with the term referring to linguistic and nonlinguistic social practices and ideological assumptions that construct power or racism (Schiffrin, Tannen, & Hamilton, 2001).

Since critical discourse analysis does not constitute a specific research direction, it does not have a unified theoretical framework. It has been applied to research on gender inequality, media discourse, political discourse, ethnocentrism, anti-Semitism, nationalism, and racism (Van Dijk, 2001). The typical vocabulary of many scholars features notions of power, dominance, hegemony, ideology, class, gender, race, discrimination, interest, reproduction, institutional social structure and social order. Power is a central notion in most critical work on discourse and more specifically the social power of groups or institutions. Social power can be defined in terms of control. The power of dominant groups may be integrated in laws, rules, norms, habits, and even in a quite general consensus, thus taking the form of hegemony.

Within discourse, narrative analysis has become one of the major areas of research (Linde, 2001). Critical discourse analysis employs inter-disciplinary techniques of text analysis to examine how texts construct representations of the world, social identities, and social relationships (Luke, 2004). Analyses of stories include line-by-line analyses of the narrative structure. Others have examined how the structure of stories reflects that of the social actions found in the stories. Still others analyze the linguistic features of this discourse genre. Some researchers are interested in how people use stories to portray sociolinguistic identities, and how narrative distributes social power and creates and perpetuates social relations.

Today increasing attention is being directed toward the political effects of narrative. Storytelling is seen not only as a way of creating community but as a resource for dominating others and for expressing solidarity, resistance and conflict. More and more, narrative is becoming a way of constructing "events" and giving them meaning. Through telling, we construct ourselves and our experiential worlds (Johnstone, 2001).

In the current study, I refer to written cases and critical autobiography as discourse units composed in a given situation by the teacher-inquirer. I regard the self-narrative genre as an opportunity for extracting meaning through language and revealing the teacher-inquirer's identity. My assumption is that language reflects social and political meanings. Hence, I rely upon Gee's (1992; 1999) definition of discourse and his view that meaning is found in actual contexts of use.

A Model for Critical Discourse Analysis

In this book I use three categories of analysis to reveal teachers' sense of professional self. Those categories were developed in a previous study (Ezer & Mevorach, 2008), in which we analyzed teacher-educators' narratives and revealed their professional identities. The three categories of analysis are as follows:

– *Positioning*: how the teacher-inquirers position themselves within the professional landscape. Positioning refers to how the narrators place themselves in the story vis-à-vis others (Kupferberg & Gilat, 2002) and with respect to their professional self. Occasionally positioning is particularly apparent in the figurative language used in the discourse.

– *Evaluation:* how the teacher-inquirers reflect upon their narratives, or, to use Labov's terminology (1972), how they evaluate episodes through the use of evaluation devices. I call these devices meta-statements (Ezer, Millet & Patkin, 2005). In these meta-statements the narrators say something "about" what is going on, as if they have been observing their lives and what happened in their lives from the outside.

– *Language use:* how the teacher-inquirers used language, or in other words, what style and common semantic fields were used.

CONCLUSION

Among the various types of self-study, this book focuses on three in particular, which echo and reverberate off one another: instructional situations case analysis, critical autobiography and action research. Each takes the form of a narrative, though every narrative has a different structure and emphasis, as will become clear. The following three chapters describe these three types of self-study. Each chapter surveys the relevant theoretical background, outlines the research strategy, and offers representative narratives from studies carried out by teacher-inquirers. These narratives are analyzed using the tools of critical discourse analysis to reveal the teacher's sense of professional self emerging from the text. Furthermore, the examples are used to substantiate the approach put forth in this book, that is, that self-study serves teacher-inquirers as a tool for professional development.

CHAPTER 3

INSTRUCTIONAL SITUATIONS CASE ANALYSIS

This chapter presents the instructional situations case analysis approach as a significant tool for the teacher-inquirer. This approach is based upon the view of the teacher as inquirer as well as on the accumulated body of knowledge about cases in teaching. Even so, I have further developed, refined and expanded the approach during the course of my work with teacher-inquirers. The approach began to take shape during a workshop I offered to teachers studying in a graduate program on Learning and Instruction (M.Ed.). The chapter describes three instructional situations as told by teacher-inquirers, each representing a different type of case. Each of the situations is described twice. The first account—the "authentic case of teaching"—recounts the situation as it actually happened. The second account—the "expected case of teaching"—describes what was hypothetically expected to occur based upon analysis of the original authentic event.

The outcome of self-study is usually assumed to be a narrative (Bullough & Pinnegar, 2004). Teachers' case stories are in fact short narratives that capture a single moment or individual events from the past that teacher-inquirers focus on from their current perspective. In this chapter, I contend that an external inquirer—in this case me—can analyze these short narratives and use them to reveal a teacher-inquirer's sense of professional self. My analysis examined the narratives from two perspectives: that of the authentic case of teaching and that of the expected case of teaching. Each of these perspectives, it seems, reveals a different side of the identity of the teacher-inquirer telling the story: the identity emerging from the event, and a virtual identity that the teacher-inquirer apparently expects and desires. I used discourse analysis of the narratives to reveal the teacher-narrator's professional self. This choice of method was based upon the assumption that critical discourse analysis facilitates exposure of professional identity, i.e., sense of professional self. The essence of this identity is found primarily in the relations among the different participants in the described narrative and the positioning of the teacher-inquirers within their professional arena or work environment. Even if the participating teachers share the same strategy in their case writing, each teacher differs from the others. Hence, each case story presented here is fundamentally different from the others, so that the sense of professional self emerging from analyzing each narrative will differ from teacher to teacher.

The chapter first introduces the theoretical background that set the stage for the case-based outlook in teaching, which in turn led to developing the instructional situations described in this chapter. It then details the model upon which this activity was implemented and the case criteria. Finally, the model is demonstrated by three actual instructional situation cases described and analyzed by teachers who participated in a graduate workshop on instructional situations case analysis. Each case is followed by my own analysis as an investigator of teacher-inquirers, with the goal of revealing the sense of professional self of teacher-inquirers as they recount their case stories.

THEORETICAL BACKGROUND

The theoretical background opens by defining the notion of a case. After that, the discussion focuses on how the case-based approach is related to teacher education. Projects from across the globe are presented to exemplify case stories developed by teachers.

What Is a Case?

During the past two decades, analysis of instructional situations using cases has become a major field in teacher education and a methodology for structuring knowledge from one's own cases and those of other educators. The approach emerges from authentic cases that take place in the instructional field. Its goal is to bridge between theoretical principles and practice and to enhance teachers' thinking. In Israel, this approach has developed under the name "case literature" (Silberstein, 2002). Implementation of the approach involves two practical modes: (a) examining the cases of others in order to stimulate reflective thinking and to learn from authentic experiences of educators, and (b) writing cases in order to help teachers understand how the world of teaching works from the inside. Each of these modes involves working with cases. The difference between them is that some of the cases are written by researchers in order to recount the teachers' narratives, while others are written by the teachers themselves in the process of their own critical analysis (Hashweh, 2004).

Silberstein (2002) defines cases as "stories about an event or a series of instructional events, dramatically, reliably and clearly documented or told by those involved. These stories are written by teachers or researchers, and they provide flash representations of problems and dilemmas from the teaching field" (p. 23). Case literature focuses primarily on analyzing events, episodes, lesson segments, incidents of teachers coping with a defined teaching problem on a specific topic (Silberstein, 2002). To further clarify, under consideration here is a collection of statements representing knowledge about teaching. Such descriptions can be short and on the mark. A story becomes a case when it can be interpreted as part of pedagogical knowledge. Thus, it becomes an important and meaningful pedagogical tool, a vehicle of academic knowledge, yet it is not a source of knowledge or lesson planning. A case is not merely a story or a narrative, but rather an instrument for fostering understanding in teaching (Carter, 1999).

Cases offer teachers the opportunity to learn how to think like teachers and to develop habits of thinking that will enhance the skills and attributes required of an education professional. Cases also facilitate the development of diverse perspectives realized in conflict situations. Moreover, they provide a framework within which teachers can develop a conceptual view of themselves as professional educators. By means of analysis and reflection, teachers become acquainted with the problematic nature and results of specific events. Cases are unique in that they enable teachers and students to see how theory works in practice. Furthermore, cases make it possible to make the connection between theory and practice in education (Goldblatt & Smith, 2005; Lundeberg, 1999; Silberstein, 2002). To reflect, to enter into a dialogical discussion with self and others, and to form a collaborative community are essential components facilitated by case discussion (Goldblatt & Smith, 2004).

Case Literature and Teacher Education

While the effectiveness of the case approach in teacher education is currently being examined, the notion of using cases as educational tools is not a new one. It has been used in training attorneys and physicians since the early 20th century (Carter, 1999). Despite the current controversy over how to educate teachers to teach in a multicultural society, all seem to agree that teacher education must be improved and professionalism must be developed and encouraged. Traditional approaches in the form of separate courses consisting of lectures and reading materials apparently are not sufficiently effective in meeting the need for teachers to continue learning over the course of their professional lives. In this context, then, we must ask why cases and methods in the field of case literature are important for teacher education.

Many consider case literature as an opportunity for teachers to reformulate what they already know and what they are capable of doing. Accordingly, they will develop analytic and problem-solving skills, acquire an instructional repertoire, enhance their reflective abilities and participate in a positive learning experience within a community of learners. Cases also present a realistic picture of the complexity of teaching and enable teachers to develop professionalism in teaching (Merseth, 1999). This type of professionalism requires teacher educators to nurture reflective and research skills (Cole & Knowles, 2000; Robinson & McMillan, 2006). Cole and Knowles (2000) claim that such professionalism can develop by means of reflexive inquiry—inquiry anchored within the context of personal history—with the goal of making a connection between personal life and professional career and of understanding personal influences on professional practice. Thus, teaching and teacher development are anchored in what is personal. Teaching is the expression of who the teachers are as individuals, of their values, beliefs, perspectives and experiences as they develop throughout their lifetime. Cole and Knowles believe that for teachers to understand their professional lives and their work and for them to develop professionally they must recognize their developmental stage as teachers as well as their ongoing experiences and the formative impact of their perspectives and practices. Metaphorically speaking, these researchers claim that being reflexive is like having a mirror and transparent prism with which to view practice. This prism breaks down the different components of practice, just like the colors of the spectrum are broken down in a glass prism. Reflexive inquiry examines all the elements of life, their diverse colors and facets, in and outside of school, and considers their implications on professional life.

Reflective and academic consideration of the events in a teacher's professional life constitutes a new and more meaningful tool in a teacher's professional development. Case literature makes this type of inquiry possible, and stimulates teachers' ability to reflectively examine their own work. Nonetheless, we must remember that cases do not teach themselves, but rather require a sensitive and experienced moderator who can help participants achieve insight and awareness (Shulman, 1996). This approach gained momentum in the late 1980s, when Shulman (1986) affirmed that case literature is important for pedagogical purposes. Indeed, case development is a powerful pedagogical strategy, for cases facilitate a more critical examination of school policies and practices that encourage learners to leave their own culture and native language outside the classroom door (Hashweh, 2004; Nieto, 1999). Cases can promote, describe and explain changes in teachers. They can also serve as ways to cross boundaries and can facilitate the integration of research and cognition/emotion, all of which are important to a teacher's professional development (Hashweh, 2004).

The use of cases promotes the following attributes among teachers: (a) theoretical and practical understanding—the ability to identify, frame and discover problems, to approach problems from a number of different perspectives, and to assess the results; (b) metacognition—thinking about awareness and about the way in which we think; (c) beliefs—teachers' beliefs affect how they interpret theories and their own instructional situations, and the relations between beliefs and practice are reciprocal and affect one another; (d) social, moral and epistemological growth—the way in which teachers view knowledge and diverse axioms provides a window on their epistemological development; (h) reasoning and substantiation—critical analysis of complex situations, identifying problems and issues, use of cognitive flexibility, reflection on practice; and (i) the exposure of indirect (latent) knowledge (Lundeberg, 1999).

Furthermore, teachers can also use cases to help develop their awareness of diverse groups of learners in a society that is primarily multicultural. In effect, the use of cases is highly relevant in a multicultural society marked by heterogeneous classrooms and different cultural representations within the class. Cases can provide educators with important information on cultural groups and enable them to construct a cultural profile of the diverse learners in the class (Nieto, 1999).

In summary, case literature has developed over the past two decades in the context of teachers who examine their own work over the course of their lifetime. This approach is seen as a preliminary approach to research as it demands that teachers be able to observe, inquire and reflect, be methodical in their observations and able to draw conclusions from their inquiries. Hence, not only do teachers examine their own work in diverse contexts (events, event segments, sequences of events), but they also can examine their instructional cases in real time, or after time has passed by relating their narratives in retrospect, as they remember them. An incident turns into a case only after the teacher has analyzed and interpreted it. This type of inquiry into the professional context empowers teachers and enables them to develop professionally based upon new insights and conclusions that can lead to new ways of behaving and responding.

Teachers' Stories in Case Literature

The body of professional literature documenting teachers' stories is growing. These stories are published in diverse types of books, ranging from those focusing on a particular topic to more eclectic books that include the instructional stories of teachers from different subject areas. In addition, numerous articles describe cooperative teaching projects, from which each participating teacher ultimately derived his or her own story. Each instructional activity is a story unto itself, and no one activity is the same as any other. Nonetheless, what connects and binds these activities is the understanding that cases constitute a tool for teachers' professional development. For example, in *Stories from the Heart*, Meyer (1996) tells the stories of prospective and practicing teachers understanding themselves as curious and literate beings. Another book, with the apt title *Stories Teachers Tell* (Hartman, 1998), reflects on the professional practice of teachers teaching diverse subject areas. In addition to the literature documenting the professional stories of teacher educators, a body of literature is also developing that focuses on collective stories in education, such as the article by Paulus, Woodside, and Ziegler (2007) that describes how personal stories from the classroom turn into group narrative.

Shulman (1996) reported on a project to encourage multiculturalism, led by a team of teachers in San Francisco. In order to develop cases, the first year of the project involved a group of teachers from diverse ethnic groups. These cases were more than mere narratives. They were actual classroom teaching cases and represented challenges raised by classroom diversity. Numerous topics were raised: the problems faced by a teacher from a cultural background different than that of the class, coping with children with limited knowledge of English, working with parents and communities from diverse cultures. Often the cases focused on the problems faced by the teacher in working with individual pupils or with groups. Issues involving racial bias, cultural status, gender and teachers' lack of experience were raised frequently. The group discussions encouraged colleagues to comment on the cases raised by the participants. In the project's second year, the workshop included a group of 15 new teachers in order to collect data and to demonstrate the role of the group facilitator. Another goal was to examine the impact of workshop participation on the participants' attitudes toward diversity. The seminar was held once a month, under laboratory conditions; each session was two hours and took place after school. Between sessions, the teachers read the instructions and the stories told by their colleagues, and noted their comments. The project analyzed the drafts of the current participants as well as those of their predecessors in the project, the minutes of the discussions, the completed questionnaires, and the written comments of the participants before and after the discussions. In addition, the participants were interviewed during the seminar.

Nieto (1999) examined a project in which friends, colleagues and doctoral students were invited to join her in identifying pupils from different cultural backgrounds. As part of the project, each participating teacher wrote up his or her professional story. As the project progressed, the participants discussed the criteria for selecting the pupils, learned about cases in the professional literature, and sought out the necessary information about the background and experience of the pupils' families. One decision was to concentrate on high school students. Another referred to the type of diversity to be included in the cases. Ten cases were decided upon, based upon practical considerations. These cases included an equal number of boys and girls, and focused on cultural, racial and linguistic diversity. Moreover, it was decided to include white pupils from unusual backgrounds, who are usually not visible when referring to multiculturalism. As a result, the project included an American Protestant girl of European origin, an American Jewish boy, and an Arab American boy. While the pupils were not selected randomly, the sample was also not planned, and no model pupil was sought. Rather, the primary criteria involved ethnic, racial and linguistic diversity as well as a mix of boys and girls. The pupils were recommended by different people, and some were even discovered by chance. The personal stories of young people are always interesting, but the facilitator sought to provide even more interesting stories for the teachers reading the cases. She wanted the teachers to understand the context of the pupils' life stories. Why did a pupil's family immigrate to the United States? Why was it important for a particular interviewee to speak his native language at home? Why did another pupil join a street gang, and why was it difficult for him to leave the gang? To answer questions such as these, the interviewing teachers needed to learn more about the history of these people. Because they felt compelled to read background material about those they interviewed, developing the cases took longer than expected. In all the cases, the background material added another dimension to the stories, leading to cases from numerous cultures: African-American, Jewish, Mexican, Puerto Rican, Vietnamese, Lebanese, Native Americans and others.

Hashweh (2004) examined a project for teaching democracy through case-based problem-solving. The study found that using cases worked. In writing up the cases, it ultimately became clear that cooperative writing was much more than merely documentation. Indeed, it was a form of shared research regarding the participants' experience. The education for democracy project began in 1998 and lasted three years. The participants comprised nine teachers from public elementary schools in Ramallah and the West Bank. The teachers met in a weekly workshop over the course of a year. At first, they were taught the philosophy and rationale of the case-based approach and its relation to education for democracy. They worked together among themselves, collaborated with university teachers and formulated a unit on cases. In the second semester, they themselves taught this unit in the

9th grade, continuing to meet once a week to reflect on their teaching. The teaching unit included a case involving punishment of pupils in school. This story served as basic material for learning about democracy, citizenship, laws, power relations, government, accountability and human rights.

During the second year, the teachers worked to formulate an additional five cases for this study unit. In the first semester of the third year, each of the teachers taught one case in the 9th through 12th grades at his or her school, using the same approach as the other teachers. In the second semester, each teacher wrote a report documenting the case with respect to his or her teaching. The teachers continued to meet on a weekly basis to reflect and consider their work.

During the project, the participants kept journals documenting their experience in teaching the unit. In their journals they documented what they had taught, keeping in mind Schwab's four commonplaces: teacher, learner, subject matter, and milieu.

As noted, the teachers met weekly to discuss their problems and to support one another. These weekly meetings proved extremely effective. The second semester meetings were devoted to discussing what the teachers had written. They talked about case significance and potential components, using the work of Shulman (1996) to assist them. They began discussing the goals of case writing and documenting their experiences in teaching democracy, and they considered how to communicate these experiences to their professional colleagues. The teachers learned that narratives have a plot and dramatic intent, and they were encouraged to write in a literary fashion. They were instructed to include four components in the case: description, interpretation, assessment and reflection. This technique, proposed by Shulman, included writing for a short period of time, reading what was written, and then writing again for a short period. After that, the teachers worked in pairs to help each other revise their first drafts. At the end of each session, a number of teachers read aloud what they had written, and received feedback from the others. The group was transformed into a community of learners learning about democracy.

Goldblatt & Smith (2004) investigated a project at The Ontario College of Teachers in Canada whose purpose was to raise awareness of standards of practice among teachers. Eighteen teachers wrote narrative descriptions of their professional work. Then, by means of reflection and cooperative examination, they constructed cases in order to examine whether standards were inherent in or missing from their practical experience. The college then invited twelve schools to participate in a workshop whose purpose was to raise awareness of standards of practice.

The sessions focused on the dilemma faced by a new teacher attempting to impress a supervisor. Participants analyzed the cases according to Judy Shulman's method. They were asked to reconstruct a personal dilemma from their own practice to create the "case nucleus." They then examined how this nucleus was related to standards of professional conduct and whether it reflected any of these standards. They also discussed the case in view of the standards. The group members found themselves assuming the roles of colleagues and editors. Indeed, listening to the stories of others appears to generate additional data about each individual's own experience.

After the participants rewrote their cases, the college facilitators edited the cases based on a more profound awareness of the importance of preserving the authentic voice of the writers. By means of reflection, all the writers were able to examine their own practice and design the case to reflect the reality of their educational dilemmas. Reflection developed as a norm for considering events and dilemmas, thus leading the teachers to think like teachers. The teachers were also empowered, for they began to believe that they are the guiding force in directing their own learning and professional development.

Ezer (2002b) focused on the story of a fifth-grade teacher. The story she told was twofold: that of a teacher coping with a pupil having trouble in class, and that of the same pupil, who managed to break out of the cycle of failure through teacher-directed and pupil-focused literacy activities. The story is subjective, as seen through the teacher's personal lens. It is the story of a teacher dealing with a pupil who has learning difficulties, whose problems are not only in understanding and expressing himself but also in listening and paying attention. As a result, the pupil has disciplinary problems in class. As stated previously, it is also the story of a child as told by the teacher and a story of hope for other children with learning difficulties. The teacher describes how she "learns who the pupil is" through a simple literacy activity in the form of a story he wrote. She tells how she devised an individual teaching program for the pupil based on his abilities and how she used this program to transform his attitude from passive to positively active, to establish his position in society and to have an impact upon his behavior in other classes as well. In sum, this case is a story of growth, not only of the pupil but also of the teacher, who was able to realize, through recalling the instructional situation, what kind of teacher she was and what actually promoted learning and transformed the attitudes of a special needs pupil.

The above survey shows that the case literature on teacher education has grown in recent years, both among student teachers and among teachers themselves. Yet each study differs depending upon the context in which it was carried out. The theoretical literature does not report on the use of case analyses for revealing professional identity or teachers' sense of professional self, which is an interesting addition to case analysis, as presented in this chapter. In the following discussion, I describe the analysis of instructional situations cases. This analysis differs from what has appeared in the theoretical literature thus far. For this purpose, the unique case analysis model developed in my classes serves as the database for analysis.

THE CASE ANALYSIS MODEL

The teacher-inquirers who participated in my instructional situation analysis workshop were asked first to document an instructional situation, i.e. a case that took place in the teachers' workplace, and then to interpret it based upon more comprehensive national, global and social circumstances. To this end, every situation or event in a teacher's professional life is perceived as an instructional situation, even if it does not actually occur within the classroom. This perception is based upon the notion that teaching involves not only providing knowledge but also educating for values, and that it takes place anytime and anywhere within the educational system.

Teachers participating in the workshop on case analysis were presented with the following goals:
- To develop as an independent teacher practitioner able to choose a topic, collect relevant information (from the theoretical literature and from events in the field), process and interpret the information, and think critically as a professional educator and an academic scholar.
- To use authentic cases (instructional situations) to learn about teaching methods and up-to-date theoretical approaches.
- To become acquainted with the relevant theoretical literature in the field of instructional situations case analysis and to examine possibilities for using this methodology for developing as a teacher-inquirer and for sharing the knowledge with other teacher colleagues within a community of learners.

Each teacher was asked to identify and investigate a case related to her own professional world. The workshop participants described in this book presented cases relating to a variety of fields, among them teacher-pupil relations (discipline, violence and the like), teacher-parent relations, teacher-administration relations, relations between mentor teacher and student teacher, integration of pupils with special needs (exceptional pupils of all sorts, new immigrants and others), children's medical problems (for example obesity among children) and sex education in school.

Stages of Inquiry

The stages of inquiry for the teacher-inquirer are as follows:
– **Writing the story as it occurred:** identifying and writing up the case.
– **Locating the dilemma or problem:** identifying the dilemma or problem emerging from the case, and defining themes for additional research in the theoretical literature.
– **Searching for professional information:** reading theoretical material based on the themes identified in the cases and writing a relevant literature survey.
– **Interpreting the cases:** providing personal interpretation based upon the theoretical issues.
– **Writing the expected story:** writing the story as the teacher-inquirer believes it should have occurred based upon her new insights, and interpreting the expected story.

The expected story offers the teacher-inquirer a "second chance" based on the "revolving door" concept that gives the teacher the opportunity to have the same experience again, this time as she would have wanted to experience it. This second chance is given to the teacher-inquirer after having already identified the event's major themes, examined them in the theoretical literature at a safe distance from the teaching situation and interpreted the incident in view of the professional knowledge of others emerging from the literature survey. The revolving door enables the teacher to re-experience the incident in a more desirable way, while using judgment based upon the evidence she collected and the rational interpretation she gave to the event. From time to time, when a critical incident occurs in her class, a teacher may find herself saying, "if only it had happened differently," not knowing why she feels this way or how exactly it should have played out. By analyzing the instructional situation using the steps outlined above, the teacher can distance herself from the event and suggest an alternative based upon academic and rational considerations.

Note that sometimes the expected story offers a negative alternative to what actually happened, especially when the authentic case was a story of success. In such a case, the teacher-inquirer presents the event from the perspective of another teacher who did not succeed, as in the third instructional situation (C) in this chapter. In contrast, in some cases a successful event can be presented from the perspective of another participant, such as a pupil or a parent. This provides the teacher-inquirer the opportunity to step into someone else's shoes, so to speak, and to experience the incident rationally through the eyes of the other, either in a successful or an unsuccessful instructional situation.

In the following discussion, each story is told by the teacher-narrator, for she is the one who is involved in the instructional situation being described. Two teachers analyzed each story: the teacher-narrator and a colleague whose job it is to interpret the story from another point of view. Hence, while each story is told by the teacher-narrator, the work is presented by a pair of teacher-inquirers.

Case Writing Criteria

The case stories presented here are based upon criteria determined by the group of teachers who participated in the workshop. Each case meets the following criteria:
– It is authentic.
– It has a clear narrative organizational structure: opens with a summary or abstract, is set in a particular context, contains a sequence of events, suggests a solution or disentanglement of the problem, and includes evaluation devices[3].
– It is interesting and trustworthy, stimulates others to identify it with their own professional lives, and is relevant professionally.
– It is written clearly, using language appropriate to written rather than spoken discourse.
– It contains a dilemma or a problem within the professional context.
– It is professionally significant to teachers.

THREE INSTRUCTIONAL SITUATIONS

In presenting the instructional situations in this section, I first describe the inquiry and analytic processes of the teacher-inquirers. In my capacity as an external investigator, I then present my own critical discourse analysis of the written stories. Discourse analysis facilitates examining the way the story is told (in other words, how the story is being told), and not just the content (in other words, what the story is about).

I have chosen three different instructional situations from the extensive inventory of cases. Each story represents a different situation, and in each of the three cases the teacher-inquirer has successfully told both the story as it indeed occurred and the expected story she believed should have occurred.

The first two cases relate to violence against teachers, while the third is about a pupil considered to be weak. Situation A is related to the teaching environment, yet takes place outside the classroom. This situation touches upon a matter that troubles many teachers—discipline, or in other words the reciprocal relations between teacher and pupils. Situation B focuses on a classroom incident in which the mother of one of the pupils is involved. The topic of the relationship between the teacher and the pupils' parents is also quite common. This specific case describes relations with a parent of an immigrant pupil, defined by the teacher-inquirers as an intercultural conflict. The teacher-narrators considered these first two situations as critical events in their professional lives and would have liked them to have been resolved differently. Situation C takes place in one of the subject area lessons in a regular junior high school class, describing how the teacher intentionally nurtures a pupil regarded by the other subject area teachers as an underachiever. The teacher deemed this ongoing and critical situation to be significant to her professional life, for she had not previously experienced anything similar and she considered it a story of success.

Each of these instructional situations—A, B and C—is described in the following order: the story as it occurred, the teacher-inquirers' interpretation of the story based upon researching the theoretical literature, and the expected story constructed out of the teacher-inquirers' newly acquired knowledge and insights. Finally, my discourse analysis of the two case stories—authentic and expected—is provided in order to reveal the sense of professional self emerging from the teacher-inquirers' written discourse.

Instructional Situation A – Hagit and Michal's Stories: A Case of Violence Against a Teacher in School[4]

As noted, the first instructional situation is about teacher-pupil relations. The story is told as it occurred by Hagit, the teacher involved. Hagit examined the incident together with her colleague Michal, so from now on I will refer to them in the plural as teacher-inquirers. After Hagit's description, the following steps taken by the teacher-inquirers are described: identifying the dilemma or problem raised, deciding upon the themes on which to seek out additional relevant information, interpreting the case story, and, finally, telling the expected story, a new scenario constructed based upon the teacher-inquirers' new understanding and insight gained from the theoretical literature and their personal interpretation of the incident.

Authentic Case of Teaching

A Blow to the Neck

This story took place around five years ago. I was on schoolyard duty. When the bell rang to end the recess, I started walking towards the school building along with the stragglers, when all of a sudden I felt an awful blow to my neck. A soccer ball kicked in my direction had whacked me in the neck. I turned around and saw a group of boys known in school as "the wild bunch" who were always getting into mischief. The school guard who was standing near them looked at me and muttered under his breath, "It was B, and he did it on purpose." I went over to B and asked him if he had kicked the ball. He said yes, and added, "It wasn't on purpose." "Okay," I said, and asked him to come with me to the principal's office.

I got to the principal's office before B so I could tell her what had happened. I briefly described the incident, stressing that the guard said B had done it on purpose. The principal listened to me and asked B to come in. She said to me, "Go teach your class. It's okay." I remained rooted in place. She repeated in a loud voice, "Go on, it's okay, I'm handling it, go back to your class."

I did what she asked, and went back to class, expecting that she'd call me back in a few minutes to clarify and handle the matter.

Even though this was clearly a matter of intentional violence that resulted in my needing six months of physical therapy treatments, the principal never discussed the matter with me. B was not punished and did not apologize. After two weeks went by, I understood that as far as the principal was concerned the matter was closed. I told myself to be real and just let it be. It's over and not important.

But it was not over.

Every time I passed by B and his gang of hooligans, they would taunt me about the whack in the neck. "Do you remember how B kicked a ball at your neck? Do you remember how hard he hit you?" This behavior clearly indicated to me that the matter had not been handled properly. By talking openly and taunting me about what had happened, the kids were only revealing what everyone already knew. B had kicked that ball at me on purpose, and had not been made to account for his behavior. Therefore, his buddies felt free to belittle what had happened and to tease me. Every time I was taunted by the pupils, I felt I had been abandoned and deserted, left alone to my own inadequate devices.

This went on for a number of months, until one day when I passed by the gang, one of them asked me, "Tell me, does your neck still hurt from that blow?" I turned around, looked B straight in the eye, and said to him, "My neck hasn't hurt me for some time now, but my heart still aches, and it will take me a lot more time to understand why you did it."That was the first time I saw any signs of remorse on B's face. I saw him squirm on the bench, and then he said, "I'm so sorry. I'm really sorry… I promise it will never happen again."

And that was the end of the story. From then on, no one ever teased me about it.

Still, I wonder about the principal's conduct. How is it that she did not express any interest in me? Why didn't she verify the matter with me and allow me to confront the pupil? Is it possible that she quietly settled matters with B without informing me? To me the principal's behavior indirectly endorsed the pupil's violent conduct and undermined my position and authority as a teacher. This had a major impact on my relations with her over the years.

Teacher-inquirers' interpretations. The teacher-inquirers identified three major themes in the case story: a) intentional pupil violence directed against a teaching employee; b) the system's handling of the case of a pupil who has injured a teaching employee; and c) teacher authority. They regarded these themes as "problems" to be clarified by reading the theoretical literature. By reading the theory concerning the above issues the teacher-inquirers gained the following insights:

Pupil violence in school: To the teacher-inquirers, it appeared that B had not planned his action in advance, and he had no reason for or intention of hurting the teacher in particular. At the end of recess, B found himself walking behind a teacher, with a soccer ball in his hand, and without thinking he aimed and kicked. Based upon their reading, the teacher-inquirers concluded this was random violence, without any clear reason. The teacher, the pupil and the ball came together at a particular time and place, and the violent act occurred. This type of violence in school can have a number of causes, among them a weakened family unit, a shortage of school resources for coping with violence, the collapse of moral education among today's youth, violence in the family, use of drugs, and exposure to violence in the media. The teacher-inquirers also noted that B came from a troubled and complicated family situation. He was being raised by his mother, a single parent who was intellectually limited, after his father had been removed from the home due to domestic violence.

Coping with violence in school: The teacher-inquirers noted that in this incident the principal's response, or more accurately her lack of response, to such an act of violence did not adhere to the law as set out in the director-general's directives, nor as it appears in school regulations. Although the principal assumed responsibility for handling this incident, she did not document it, did not hold any discussions with the teacher who had been hurt, and did not ask about her welfare. She also did not inform the parents, the school staff or the supervisory bodies. The teacher-inquirers hence concluded there was no intervention by the system. This conclusion goes along with what the theoretical literature terms an attempt by the system "to sweep things under the rug." A principal's management style is closely tied to the school's organizational climate.

Teacher authority: In interpreting the issue of teacher authority, the teacher-inquirers discussed the distribution of power and authority in school and the organizational culture. Their interpretation was based upon the work of researchers, according to whom violence in the form of annoying or harming a teacher constitutes a challenge to the accepted order of things, leading to a new order in which the attacking pupil assumes a position of strength in confronting the teacher whose status as an authority figure has been undermined. The teacher-inquirers saw the results of this incident in terms of a situation in which the teacher is alone in the system and must cope by herself with incidents such as those described in the case. According to them, restoring teacher-pupil relations usually means giving pupils a second chance. They believe that relations must be improved to restore the undermined authority of the teacher who was the victim of violence. In the story described here, the teacher involved ignored the gang's repeated taunting out of a clear feeling that the system would not support her and that she was on her own.

After completing their interpretations and gaining new insights, the teacher-inquirers began writing the expected story. While they understood the importance of using power and authority reasonably and wisely rather than automatically, it was difficult for them not to wonder about the principal's behavior, which led to the teacher having to cope with a gang of hooligans at school. They pointed to the physical and emotional price the teacher had to pay. In their view, any teacher victimized by violence that was not properly handled would have to pay the same price. They believed that not handling such incidents would harm the entire system and lead to an undermining of teacher authority.

Expected case of teaching. The teacher's version of the expected story describes how the same violent incident could have been reasonably handled while maintaining clear boundaries and safeguarding the teacher's authority and the dignity of all involved.

I Saw Remorse in His Eyes

This story took place around five years ago. I was on schoolyard duty. When the bell rang to end the recess, I started walking towards the school building along with the stragglers, when all of a sudden I felt an awful blow to my neck. A soccer ball kicked in my direction had whacked me in the neck. I turned around and saw a group of boys known in school as "the wild bunch" who were always getting into mischief. The school guard who was standing near them looked at me and muttered under his breath, "It was B, and he did it on purpose." I went over to B and asked him if he had kicked the ball. He said yes, and added, "It wasn't on purpose." "Okay," I said, and asked him to come with me to the principal's office.

Together we went to the principal's office, and I briefly described the incident. The principal listened to the story. She then told me to go to the teachers' room to calm down, and asked a teacher who was free to cover for me in my classroom. She told B to stay in her office until she clarified what had happened. Looking a bit worried, the principal went out and made me a cup of tea and asked me to wait until the pain in my neck subsided. All this time B sat terrified in the principal's office, waiting to be called.

After half an hour, when the pain had subsided somewhat, the principal, after again asking how I was feeling, tried to determine what had happened and asked me to fill out an incident report as soon as I felt up to it. She then told me that the guard, who had been playing soccer with the pupils at recess, claimed that nothing had preceded the kick and that it had been aimed at me on purpose. She went on to say that B did not deny what had happened, but insisted he had not meant to hurt me. He just kicked the ball and it happened to hit me. B went back to his class. The principal told me she set up an emergency meeting with the school psychologist, the assistant principal, the school counselor and B's homeroom teacher to decide what should be done next since she had no intention of letting this matter go. She also asked B's parents to come to school the next day.

That week, the incident was discussed by the school's multiprofessional team, and the incident details were reported to the staff, B's parents and the school's supervisory board. Due to B's complicated family situation, the team unanimously decided not to expel him. After I was consulted, it was decided that for the next week B would spend recess on detention working in the library.

During recess one day, while B was arranging books on the shelf, he suddenly turned toward me and asked, "Tell me, does your neck still hurt from that blow?" I lifted my head, looked B straight in the eye, and said to him, "My neck hasn't hurt me for some time now, but my heart still aches, and it will take me a lot more time to understand why you did it." I saw remorse on B's face. He sat down, squirmed on the chair, lowered his eyes, and said, "I'm so sorry. I'm really sorry... I promise it will never happen again."

His remorse was sincere and genuine. I asked the principal to reduce his punishment by a third for good behavior.

This new scenario is what the teacher-inquirers expected to happen based upon what they read in the theoretical literature about school violence and how to cope with it, as well as about teacher authority.

The new incident starts out just like what actually happened (the authentic story). The stories begin to diverge in how the principal handles the incident. In the expected story, the principal pays attention to what the teacher has to say, attempts to clarify what happened by talking to the teacher and to the pupil, brings the matter up for discussion to the school's multiprofessional team (administration, counselor, homeroom teacher, psychologist), and informs the parents. At the end of the story, the teacher-inquirers take a stance regarding what the pupil did, and the pupil expresses remorse.

Readers will probably now find themselves thinking that the events in the expected story reflect every teacher's wishful thinking, and that the story is told only from the teacher's perspective. Since this is a teacher's self-study, of course the interpretation is from her perspective, and of course she is subjective. Nevertheless, the process of analyzing an instructional situation distances the teacher-inquirer from the incident itself. She is able to observe the event from the perspective of time and to interpret it using professional and academic tools, rather than the emotional and one-sided means at hand on the scene and at the time of the incident, especially one that is so personally painful. These professional tools include reflection, which cannot take place in real time but only after some time has gone by;

systematic derivation of the dilemma or problems (themes) emerging from the incident; reading professional material relevant to the identified problems; and interpretation by means of ideas derived objectively and independent of the described incident. All these methods enable the teacher-inquirer to take a step back and examine the reality of her professional life through the lens of academic and systematic observation rather than based upon emotional and associative thinking, and then to draw conclusions about what happened. The expected story can also enable the readers to accept and understand that teachers must examine violent incidents within the broader context – in this case the family background of the pupil who kicked the ball. Clearly, the bulk of the teacher-inquirer's anger is directed not at the pupil who kicked the ball, but rather at the school principal, who in her opinion did not handle the incident properly.

Sense of professional self emerging from the cases. The previous section presented a case of violence against a teacher as it occurred (authentic case) and as it was expected to occur (expected case) and demonstrated how the model of inquiry works. This section examines how the stories were told, applying discourse analysis to the authentic and expected stories. The model of analysis is based upon three aspects of critical discourse with the aim of revealing teachers' sense of professional self, (see Chapter 2 for details): positioning, evaluation and use of language.

Critical discourse analysis of authentic case of teaching . **Positioning:** In telling the story, the teacher positions herself with respect to a number of relevant people in her workplace: the school principal, the pupils involved and the pupil who actually hit her with the ball.

Towards the principal, the teacher places herself in the position of someone of lower rank, someone who must obey authority. This positioning is evident from the following statements: "I did what she asked . . . ."; "I understood that as far as the principal was concerned the matter was closed. I told myself to be real and just let it be. It's over and not important." In practice, the teacher has positioned herself as someone cut off from the principal. This separation is evident in the following statements, which cast suspicion on the principal's observable and implied way of handling the matter: "Is it possible that she quietly settled matters with B without informing me?" The separation is also apparent in the teacher's dichotomous position toward the situation. On the one hand, she expected the principal to handle the matter properly: "[I] went back to class, expecting that she'd call me back in a few minutes to clarify and handle the matter." On the other hand, the story emphasized that there was no communication whatsoever between the two with respect to this incident: ". . . the principal never discussed the matter with me."

With respect to the other pupils involved in the incident, the teacher positions herself as someone who should be an authority figure for them simply because she is a teacher, but in practice her position is actually the opposite, because they were the ones who taunted her. Thus the accepted norm was violated, and her authority turned into a lack of authority. Throughout the story, she considered her position with respect to these pupils as abnormal: "Therefore, his buddies felt free to belittle what had happened and to tease me. Every time I was taunted by the pupils, I felt I had been abandoned and deserted, left alone to my own inadequate devices."

The teacher's positioning with respect to the pupil who kicked the ball was one of ambivalence. On the one hand, she is the authority figure, and he violated that authority, as explained above with respect to his friends. On the other hand, because she considers herself as someone whose authority has been undermined, she acts to restore her authority and dignity as a human being. In this capacity of one human being to another, without taking power relations into consideration, she makes the following statement: "I turned around, looked B straight in the eye, and said to him . . . ." What she then says to him is on the same level, equal to equal: "My neck hasn't hurt me for some time now, but my heart still aches, and it will take me a lot more time to understand why you did it." In this same capacity, she also says the following: "That was the first time I saw any signs of remorse on B's face. I saw him squirm on the bench . . . ."

Evaluation: The teacher-narrator uses several devices of evaluation: adjectives indicating her one-sided position, meta-cognitive statements and qualifiers reflecting her point of view, and rhetorical questions. Following are some examples of how she used these devices in the story. The blow to her neck was "awful" (adjective reflecting the narrator's explicit opinion), and she was taunted by "a group of boys known in school as 'the wild bunch' who were always getting into mischief." According to her, the incident was "clearly a matter of intentional violence." Her personal point of view comes through in her use of the word "clearly" (a grammatical qualifier) and the adjective "intentional" to describe the violence. She also explicitly describes her feelings: "I felt I had been abandoned and deserted, left alone to my own inadequate devices." The narrator also uses the story's coda as an evaluation technique, one that summarizes the burden she is left with as a result of this incident. "To me the principal's behavior indirectly endorsed the pupil's violent conduct and undermined my position and authority as a teacher. This had a major impact on my relations with her over the years." For her, this is the main point of her story. The rhetorical questions at the end of the story also function as meta-cognitive statements and an evaluation device reflecting the teacher's positioning: "How is it that she did not express any interest in me? Why didn't she verify the matter with me and allow me to confront the pupil? Is it possible that she quietly settled matters with B without informing me?"

Language: The teacher-narrator's language is evident in the choice of words, as in those used in the story's title, the difference in syntactic structure between the first and second parts of the story, the numerous verbs of emotion and the use of metaphor, as detailed below.

The narrator already takes a stance in the story's title by choosing a short phrase taken from the story: "a blow to the neck." In Hebrew, this phrase— *"hatafti bomba batsavar"* (literally, I was hit in the neck)—uses two highly charged words in Israeli slang, thus already indicating that some sort of violence was involved. This choice of words places the narrator at the center and moves her injury to the forefront of the story.

In describing the events in the first half of the story, the teacher-narrator mainly uses short sentences marked by a single verb and a lack of adjectives. Such sentences may reflect her state of mind, in which she is focused on the events of the story. These short sentences may be the product of her desire to provide a reliable and somewhat objective rendition of what happened. On the other hand, they also reflect the emotional turbulence inherent in the rapid and staccato pace generated by these short sentences: "I described . . . stressing . . . listened to me . . . said to me . . . was not punished and did not apologize . . . ."

The last three paragraphs, beginning with "But it was not over," have a different syntactic structure. The sentence "But it was not over" serves as a pivot around which the story revolves. The description becomes richer, and the sentences longer and more syntactically complex, as in the following sentence for example: "This went on for a number of months, until one day when I passed by the gang, one of them asked me . . . ." Here the pace has changed, apparently reflecting a different state of mind.

"My heart still aches" is one of the major metaphors used to describe the teacher-narrator's emotions. Another descriptive phrase, "who were always getting into mischief," represents another strong statement on the part of the teacher. Other descriptive phrases include "the wild bunch" to describe the gang of kids involved in the incident, and the figurative phrase "I remained rooted in place" to describe the teacher's astonishment at the principal's lack of response.

Emotionally loaded slang expressions play a major role in the teacher-narrator's discourse, relaying a feeling of injury and profound insult: "I understood that as far as the principal was concerned *the matter was closed*; "*be real* and just let it be." The loaded use of high register language has the same effect. The phrasing "I felt I had been abandoned and deserted, left alone to my own inadequate devices" stresses the depth of the narrator's feelings of hurt and abandonment. This mixture of slang and high register language perhaps expresses the depth of the emotions and the teacher's intention to appeal to "everyone" no matter what his or her linguistic level. In this linguistic mixture, she seems to be submerging herself within the country's broad social context rather than within her professional context as a teacher and educator, which should be consistent with high, or at the very least normative, linguistic usage.

Generally speaking, the discourse analysis reveals both the individual "self" and the professional "self" emerging from the authentic story. On the explicit level the professional self is depicted as one that should have authority as a teacher. This authority, however, has been undermined, both by the pupils' actions and by the lack of response from the principal. The principal is the most senior authority figure in the professional organization where the teacher works, and the teacher expected to receive her full support according to accepted procedures rather than a response that deviated from system norms. The narrator's evaluation devices reflect her professional self, which takes a stance regarding pupil violence and casts doubts on how the system functioned in this case. Her individual self emerges through the many expressions of emotion and the manner in which she positions herself with respect to the pupils, particularly the one that hurt her. Here her vulnerability as a human being is revealed, as someone whose "heart still aches" over what happened, even if the physical pain is long past.

Critical discourse analysis of expected case of teaching. When constructing the expected case, the teacher-narrator used the same opening paragraph as in the authentic case because the incident is the same. The change in the expected story begins in the second paragraph, and therefore, this is where I begin the discourse analysis.

Positioning: As in her rendition of the first story, the teacher positions herself with respect to the school principal and the pupil who kicked the ball. Both were key figures in the previous story, and therefore in the expected story. The group of boys who were always getting into mischief is no longer referred to. Instead, a new group, missing from the original story, is introduced here: the school's multiprofessional team.

The teacher positions herself as someone whom the principal, in her role as a leading figure at the school, cares about. This caring attitude is expressed by the principal's behavior toward the teacher after the incident occurs: "The principal listened . . . told me to go to the teachers' room to calm down . . . made me a cup of tea . . . again asked how I was feeling . . . tried to determine what had happened . . . ." With respect to the pupil who kicked the ball, the teacher positions herself as an authority figure that cares. The child is described as "terrified" in view of what he has done, and as someone who approaches the teacher submissively, knowing she is a teacher who cares. He asks about her welfare. "Tell me, does your neck still hurt from that blow?" In keeping with his position as a pupil, he "lowered his eyes, and said, 'I'm so sorry . . . .'" With respect to her colleagues on the teaching staff, the teacher places herself within the professional community, in a collaborative role: "the team unanimously decided . . . after I was consulted . . . ."

Overall, the positioning in this story—both of the teacher toward the various participants in the story and among the participants themselves—is one of caring and concern, reflecting collaboration among those engaged in education.

Evaluation: It is interesting to note that the teacher-narrator uses few evaluation devices in the expected story. The story is told as a sequence of events as they should have occurred, with the narrator barely taking a stand. On occasion she does use descriptive words reflecting her opinion: "B sat *terrified . . . ,*" the principal looked "*a bit worried . . . ,*" he "*squirmed* on the chair . . . ." At the end of the story, the narrator's point of view is clearly reflected in the following sentence: "His remorse was sincere and genuine." In this evaluation she points at the main message of the story.

Language: The narrator's choice of words for the story's title immediately reflects the story's general direction and sets forth the teacher's point of view and the major importance of educating the pupil: "I Saw Remorse in His Eyes." The language of the story reflects a flexible and forgiving state of mind, marked by long and complex sentences such as the following. "After half an hour, when the pain had subsided somewhat, the principal, after again asking how I was feeling, tried to determine what had happened and asked me to fill out an incident report as soon as I felt up to it." The text no longer has the staccato rhythm of short sentences, as in the first story.

The language is also marked by verbs expressing caring and acceptance, such as "The principal *listened* to the story . . . "; she "*made me* a cup of tea . . . "; she again asked "*how I was feeling* . . . ." Moreover, the text uses compound predicates, which usually indicate an ongoing process: ". . . *told* me *to go to* the teachers' room to *calm down* . . . "; she "*went* out and *made* me a cup of tea"; "the team unanimously *decided* not *to expel* him."

In conclusion, the case story as it occurred is a story of injury and hard feelings told by the teacher involved in the incident. The discourse analysis uncovers the narrator's state of mind, and exposes her personal and professional sense of self during the course of the event. The event's description is marked by short sentences that lend a rapid pace to her words, the use of numerous verbs and the omission of descriptive language, thus creating a sparse and matter-of-fact language. The story also includes evaluation expressions, all directed at describing the narrator's own position of hurt and protest with respect to the violent incident and the improper way the system handled it. The teacher's choice of a title is also significant. "A Blow to the Neck" calls attention to the centrality of the event and the sense of injury in the teacher's story. The teacher-narrator positions herself with respect to three groups involved in the event: the principal, the bunch of kids and the pupil who kicked the ball. In the expected story, the events unravel as the teacher-narrator would have wanted them to happen. The language, which essentially reveals a process, is soft in its style and richer in its descriptions. It reflects appeasement, acceptance, caring and concern of all the participants, who used the same style in addressing the teacher involved in the event and in speaking to one another. The teacher-narrator uses almost no external expressions of evaluation, with the exception of the sentence summarizing the story's coda, in which she explicitly expresses her point of view. The reason for this is that the entire story as it unfolds is told from her perspective, and therefore does not need evaluative expressions. The teacher-narrator positions herself differently than in the original story, particularly with respect to the school's multi-professional team, which does not even appear in the first rendition. Her position is one of an equal among equals vis-à-vis the team's actions and decisions. In comparing the expected story to the authentic story, the choice of the title is particularly interesting. "I Saw Remorse in His Eyes" refers to the conclusion of the incident. It gives the conflict a sense of closure while placing the child at the center. In a way, the expected story reveals a different teacher with an alternative sense of professional self: a teacher at peace with herself, one whose job is to educate the pupils and not to self-indulge in her personal problems, a teacher whose role at school is to show concern while placing the pupil at the center of the educational enterprise.

Instructional Situation B: The "Promised" Land?[5]

As noted above, the second instructional situation focuses on teacher-parent relations.[6] In this case, the parent happens to be a new immigrant from the former Soviet Union.

Authentic Case of Teaching

I teach in a school in south Tel Aviv. The school has approximately 200 pupils, ranging from kindergarten to 6th grade. For the past ten years, I've been a first grade teacher in the school's early childhood unit[7]. My class has 17 pupils and one teacher's aide who is working with first graders for the first time this year. Most of the pupils in the school speak Russian at home and come from low socioeconomic backgrounds. They are not highly motivated to learn and often behave violently, both physically and verbally. The parents are only minimally involved in their children's education, usually when their child complains of being the victim of violence.

The case I am describing took place this year.

One morning when the bell rang at 8:00, the mother of H, one of the girls in my class, burst into the classroom in a fit of emotions. She began screaming in Russian that her daughter H was afraid to come to school due to the excessive violence there.... Because her outburst was in front of all the children, I told her to leave the room so we could discuss the problem outside the class. She refused to leave and began screaming in Russian peppered with garbled Hebrew that she no longer wanted her daughter in this school and that she would wait for the boy who had hit her to "teach him a lesson." Again I tried explaining that her behavior was inappropriate and that she was not allowed to scream at the children in the class, but she refused to listen. H looked uneasy. She started to cry and ran into her mother's arms.

During this entire incident the teacher's aide stood by the door and did nothing. I hinted repeatedly that I wanted her to escort the mother out of the classroom so I could calm down the children, who in the meantime had begun to get restless. The aide, a helpless look on her face, tried unsuccessfully to talk to the mother. The mother refused to leave the classroom, claiming she was waiting for the boy that had hit her daughter, who in the meantime had shown up. H's mother began yelling at him in Russian. The boy shrank into his seat, the smile disappeared from his face and he began stuttering. I asked the aide to go get the mediator, a Russian-speaking woman who acted as intermediary between the teachers and the Russian-speaking parents, or to get someone from the administration to take care of this situation. Ten minutes later, the principal of the early childhood unit showed up and tried to calm the mother down.

The mother left the classroom together with her daughter to talk to the principal, who tried to explain that her behavior had been unacceptable and that in case of a problem she should have talked to the classroom teacher and not yelled at the children. Half an hour later, H returned to the classroom with an apologetic look on her face.

I felt my class had been seriously disrupted, that its equilibrium had been violated. How could I have allowed an outsider to scream at one of the children??? I felt obligated to discuss the incident with the children and to let them know in no uncertain terms that their parents were not allowed to threaten a child on school premises—it's against the law.

During recess, I told the story to the mediator and demanded that she call in the mother for an urgent conference so that such an incident would not be repeated. The mediator set up an appointment with the mother for Friday of that same week.

At the conference, I made it clear to the mother that her behavior had been inappropriate and unacceptable. I explained the school's procedures for handling violent incidents and told her how she should have proceeded. The mother told me she was a single mother raising H on her own and that her outburst had been caused by her ongoing frustration. She promised it would not happen again.

Teacher-inquirers' interpretations. The teacher-inquirers identified the problem in the described case as a problem in parent-teacher relations, specifically related to a clash between cultures as the mother was a new immigrant from the former Soviet Union. Hence, in researching the theoretical literature they were guided by the following themes: reciprocal parent-teacher relations and culture clash.

Reciprocal parent-teacher relations: Based on their reading the teacher-inquirers classified the various approaches to parental involvement as follows: parents as observers, parents as service providers, parents as learners, parents as partners in the educational process and parents as goal-setters and decision-makers. They positioned H's mother as a parent who sees herself as involved and as a partner to the educational process because she was interested in her daughter's well-being but not necessarily in the school as an organization. The teacher-inquirers considered the possibility that parental involvement is liable to be negative and not effective, as in this case when the mother burst into the classroom and demanded to "take care of" the boy who hit her daughter (quotation marks appear in the teacher-inquirers' original work). They saw that mounting social problems such as discrimination and violence can cause parents to intervene. This was what happened with the mother involved in this case. Their review of the theoretical literature led them to the following conclusions. "Parents are active and involved in their children's education for a number of reasons. This mother apparently sensed her daughter had been harmed by violent behavior and instinctively felt the need to act immediately 'like a lioness protecting her cubs.' She did not attempt to clarify the circumstances surrounding the incident before she acted as she did." Thus, they asked themselves the following. "Why did she behave that way? Why didn't she clarify matters with the principal before her 'outburst' in the classroom?" These questions led them to think that "maybe the answer lies in her being a new immigrant from the former Soviet Union and unfamiliar with the school's rules of conduct." Based upon this line of thinking, they began searching for information about culture clash and its significance in explaining the mother's behavior.

Culture clash: The teacher-inquirers surveyed the literature on difficulties encountered by immigrants, among them language problems, motivation for social integration and adaptation to the new culture. They raised the notion of "culture shock" and pointed to the complexity of structuring a cultural identity when moving from one culture to another. The theoretical background enabled them to understand that "life is not easy for new immigrants, and perhaps the mother's behavior is a direct outcome of the frustrations she experiences as a new immigrant in Israel, a place she believes has not been hospitable to her." Therefore, they felt they "must delve more deeply into the literature and examine how new immigrants adapt to Israeli educational settings so that we can understand the circumstances surrounding the behavior of the two women involved in this incident, the teacher and the mother." They concluded that "reviewing the literature helps mainly in analyzing and understanding situations in which changing or preserving cultural identity produces tension between immigrant parents and society's agents of socialization [such as teachers and other educators]." They based their investigation on the argument that "some of these [cultural disparities] involve differing perceptions of how to nurture the child. These disparities can produce conflicts between the educational system and the immigrants."

In contrast, they also put forward the educational system's perspective as it emerged from the theoretical literature. According to the teacher-inquirers, "a lack of awareness of cultural differences can cause mis-understandings and misinterpretations of intentions and behaviors and can produce tension. In addition, teachers who are unaware of the different expectations and perceptions of immigrant parents are a source of frustration because the parents are liable to criticize the teachers' actions without the ability to understand the reasons for these actions, as in the case described above." After reviewing the relevant literature, the teacher-inquirers understood that "the mother's behavior in this case [. . . the mother refused to leave and began screaming in Russian peppered with garbled Hebrew . . . but she refused to listen] stemmed from her inability to understand what the teacher was saying." The literature also indicated that "in single-parent households the sole breadwinner must meet all the family's needs and therefore has difficulty devoting time to learning the language and garnering knowledge about everyday life." As H's mother pointed out to the teacher, "she was raising H on her own and her outburst was the result of her ongoing frustration." In view of the above, the teacher-inquirers concluded that "teachers should be exposed to cultural differences and diverse approaches to education in order to help them [the teachers] cope with the challenge of integrating this important population group." The teacher-inquirers concluded their interpretation by stating that "based upon the literature, the teacher [described in the authentic case] could have acted differently." This conclusion led them to write their expected story.

Expected case of teaching. In the expected story, the teacher-inquirers describe how the teacher could have responded to the mother's outburst. The story offers a different scenario for the incident based upon the insights gained by the teacher-inquirers in their literature survey.

I teach in a school in south Tel Aviv. The school has approximately 200 pupils, ranging from kindergarten to 6th grade. Most of the pupils in the school speak Russian at home and come from low socioeconomic backgrounds. They are not highly motivated to learn and often behave violently, both physically and verbally. For the past ten years, I've been a first grade teacher in the school's early childhood unit. My class has 17 pupils and one teacher's aide who is working with first graders for the first time this year.

One morning when the bell rang at 8:00, the mother of H, one of the girls in my class, burst into the classroom in a fit of emotions. She began screaming in Russian that her daughter H was afraid to come to school due to the excessive violence there. Because her outburst was in front of all the children, I asked her to leave the room and discuss the problem outside the class. She refused to leave and began screaming in Russian peppered with garbled Hebrew that she no longer wanted her daughter in this school and that she would wait for the boy who had hit her and "teach him a lesson." Again I tried explaining that her behavior was not appropriate and that she was not allowed to scream at the children in the class, but I saw that Hebrew did not come easily to her. I moved towards her to calm her down, and I asked the aide to take over the class so I could exchange a few words with the mother. I asked H to tell her mother to come out to talk to me so we could determine what had happened.

H, pleased with the attention I was giving her, explained what I had said to her mother. And so the three of us set off towards the teachers' room, where I offered the mother a drink of cold water. We sat in a corner and tried to talk, with H acting as interpreter. I tried to be sympathetic about the mother's distress. I told her I understood why she had burst into the classroom while at the same time explaining the school regulations. I explained that her behavior made the children in the class feel insecure and afraid. I let her know that whenever she had a problem she could come speak to me or to the mediator, a Russian-speaking woman who acted as intermediary between the teachers and the Russian-speaking parents, and that we would do our utmost to solve the problem. At the end of our conversation, I gave her the mediator's telephone number and asked her to be in touch to set up an appointment. The mother was satisfied with the individual attention she had been given. She thanked me and left the teachers' room with a broad smile on her face. I held H's hand, and together we went back to class. I felt the need to discuss this matter with the entire class and began by asking them a general question. "How do you feel? Do you want to talk about what happened?" I needed to give them a chance to openly and freely express their emotions and feelings about what had happened. I wanted to restore their sense of security and to ensure them that I would always be there for them. I also planned future activities for preventing violence, among them parent-child activities and an information sheet for the parents, in Hebrew and Russian, outlining the procedures in case of violent incidents and informing them of the role of the school mediator.

The teacher-inquirers constructed their story of the expected case based upon what they read about parent-teacher relations, and particularly in light of their new insights into the difficulties of immigrants and the relations between new immigrant parents and the Israeli school system. Though the opening of the story is similar to that of the original story, it lacks the judgmental contextual statement about the parents of immigrant children that was present in the first story. The story's description of how the mother burst into the classroom is similar to what actually happened as described in the first story. The turning point in the expected story begins after the mother fails to heed the teacher's request to step outside to clarify what happened. Unlike in the authentic story, here the teacher responds by taking things under her control. She understands that the mother is suspicious of the Israeli school system and is trying to protect her daughter, and further that the mother does not have sufficient knowledge of Hebrew to understand what the teacher is saying. In conducting herself in this manner, the teacher is looking through the multicultural lens of understanding the "other" rather than acting out of a sense of affront to her authority as a teacher, as in the first story.

The expected story does not present another one-sided position of a teacher whose authority has been undermined by a parent in front of the entire class, but rather the perspective of an educator who understands that the new immigrant parent standing before her is facing many difficulties and is in need of an empathetic response from the teacher. The girl also plays a role in the expected story, this time as a full partner to what happens in that she serves as an interpreter between the teacher and her mother. Rather than turning to an outside mediator, the teacher herself acted as mediator out of her understanding that this cultural clash was more difficult for the new immigrant mother than for an experienced teacher like herself. Because the teacher assumes the role of educator in the expected story, the other children in the class are not overlooked. The teacher makes sure to use this incident as an authentic means for venting emotions and for nurturing tolerance. The story ends by widening the circle of those involved. The teacher uses the incident to communicate, in Hebrew and Russian, with all the parents in an attempt to build a bridge of understanding between what she, the teacher, represents, and the culture of the parents, whether native-born Israelis or new immigrants.

Sense of professional self emerging from the cases. In the previous section, the authentic case story and the expected story were analyzed with respect to communication between a teacher and a new immigrant mother. This section applies discourse analysis to the manner in which the stories were told in order to reveal the sense of professional self of the teacher involved in the incident. Each story is analyzed according to the three components of discourse analysis: positioning, evaluation and use of language.

Critical discourse analysis of authentic case of teaching. The authentic case story opens by setting the context in which it occurs: the school's location, the composition of the school's pupil population and the grade taught by the teacher-narrator. In addition, the teacher-narrator describes the family background typical of most parents of the new immigrant pupils. The problems are then presented, that of the mother who has burst into the classroom and that of the teacher's aide who does not assist the teacher. The problem posed by the mother is resolved only after the teacher has asked the mediator to set up a conference. The story ends with a meeting between the teacher and the mother in the presence of the school mediator, at which time the mother promises such an incident will not happen again.

Positioning: Throughout the story of the authentic case of teaching, the teacher-narrator positions herself as a figure of authority by virtue of her being a teacher, the figure who plays the major role in the children's education in the classroom and in the school. This positioning is vis-à-vis the three major figures in the story: the mother, the aide and the mediator. It is interesting to note how the teacher-narrator positions the mother. At the very beginning of the story, the teacher places the mother within the context of the Russian-speaking community with its low socioeconomic status, those who are "only minimally involved in their children's education, primarily when their child complains of being the victim of violence." In contrast, she positions herself as a teacher who judges the mother's behavior harshly. Hence, the mother's behavior is described as an outburst of screaming. From this position of authority, the teacher "tried explaining that her behavior was not appropriate and that she was not allowed to scream at the children in the class." Yet because of the lack of communication between the teacher who is the authority figure and the mother who doesn't understand a thing about education, "she [the mother] refused to listen." Thus the conflict between the teacher and the mother is exposed.

The teacher also positions herself with respect to two other characters in the story, as mentioned before: the aide and the mediator. Vis-à-vis the aide, the teacher also places herself in a position of authority. Under the circumstances, the teacher expected the aide to act, but "the teacher's aide stood by the door and did nothing." The aide seemed helpless even though the teacher, from her position of authority, "hinted repeatedly that I wanted her to escort the mother out of the classroom so I could calm down the children." When the aide did try to talk to the mother, she was "unsuccessful" in the teacher's view. With respect to the mediator, the teacher also places herself in a position of authority. In her capacity as teacher, she makes demands of the mediator and tells her how to act. "I demanded that she call in the mother for an urgent conference so that this incident would not be repeated . . . ."

Evaluation: The narrator uses a number of obvious means of evaluation in her choice of descriptions, such as her direct statements "about the situation." Among the descriptions pointing to the narrator's judgmental position are the following: "*a flurry of emotions*"; "*garbled* Hebrew"; "*behavior[that] is inappropriate*"; "*looked uneasy*"; "The aide, *a helpless look on her face*, tried unsuccessfully to talk . . . "; "The boy *shrank* into his seat." Her position is clearly expressed in this direct statement: "I felt my class had been seriously disrupted, that its equilibrium had been violated." She also used the following rhetorical question as a means of evaluation: "How could I have allowed an outsider to scream at one of the children???"[8]

Language: The title of the story, "The 'Promised' Land?" is in the form of a question, thus directing the reader to the story's two layers: the importance of immigration to Israel, and on the other hand the problematic nature of this immigration, and more specifically the problems inherent in intercultural conflict.

In most of the linguistic expressions used in this story, the verbs are in the active form. The teacher-narrator uses a preponderance of judgmental verbs and nouns to express her position: "began *screaming*"; "*burst* into the classroom"; "She *refused* to leave." Someone else telling the same story might have chosen different verbs to describe the situation.

Many of the sentences in the case story begin with a didactic, "school-teacherish" tone that emphasizes the narrator's authoritative viewpoint. This authoritative tone is expressed through the use of authoritative-didactic verbal phrases, such as these italicized words and phrases:

I *told* her [the mother] to leave the room;

I tried explaining . . . that *she was not allowed to scream* at the children in the class;

I hinted repeatedly that I *wanted* . . . ;

I asked the aide *to go get* the mediator;

I felt obligated to discuss the incident with the children and *to let them know* . . . that their parents are not allowed . . . ;

I . . . *demanded* that she [the mediator] call in the mother . . . ;

At the conference, *I made it clear* to the mother . . . .

To summarize, the teacher-narrator's positioning vis-à-vis the other characters in the story, the means of evaluation she uses and the language she chooses together paint the picture of a teacher who is deeply rooted in her role as "schoolteacher." That is, she is the authority figure, she is the standard bearer for education in her class and her school, and she knows how instructional situations such as the one described in the story should transpire. Her sense of professional self is that of a teacher with authority who knows what to expect in teaching and is convinced that she is the one in control of her classroom environment. She knows how to "educate" and how to manage her classroom.

Critical discourse analysis of expected case of teaching. The expected story also includes an opening that describes the context in which the incident occurred. It presents the problem of the mother who has burst into the classroom and the teacher's unsuccessful attempt to calm her down in front of the class. In the expected story, the aide is not mentioned in the context of her failure to provide assistance, but rather only as someone whose role in the story is to fill in so the teacher can leave the classroom to talk to the mother. It is the teacher who suggests the problem's solution, and not the outside figure of the mediator, as in the first story. The first paragraph and half of the second paragraph are almost identical to the two opening paragraphs of the authentic story. The difference in the openings of the two stories lies in the omission of the context referring to the new immigrant mother's background. The turning point in the expected story begins with the sentence "Again I tried explaining . . . " in the second half of the second paragraph. From this point on, the second story differs from the first. The discourse analysis begins at this point.

Positioning: In the expected story, the teacher positions herself with respect to the mother, the pupil involved in the story, the pupils in the class and the pupils' parents. The role of the aide is more limited in this version, and the role of the mediator is minimized, while the pupils in the class and their parents are added as characters in the story. On the one hand, the teacher positions herself as an authority figure vis-à-vis all the characters in the story by virtue of being the teacher of this class, someone whose job is to solve problems with pupils and their parents. On the other hand, she is an understanding and supportive teacher who places concern and caring at the top of her list.

Towards the mother, the teacher places herself in a position of strength as a leader and authority figure, but also as a soothing influence. She understands the mother and is capable of showing empathy towards her: "I saw that Hebrew did not come easily to her." She therefore acts in an empathetic and calming manner:

I moved towards her to calm her down .... I told her I understood why she had burst into the classroom .... I explained that her behavior made the children in the class feel insecure and afraid. I let her know that whenever she had a problem she could come speak to me or to the mediator ....

With respect to the pupil H, the teacher places herself as an authority figure, but also as someone who cares and is concerned and who involves H in what is going on: "I asked H to tell her mother to come out to talk to me so we could determine what had happened ...." At the end of the meeting, "I held H's hand, and together we went back to class."

The teacher positions herself similarly with respect to *the other pupils in the class.* She is an authority figure for them: "I needed to give them a chance to openly and freely express their emotions and feelings ...." Yet she is also supportive: "I wanted to restore their sense of security and to ensure them that I am always there for them."

Her positioning towards *the parents* is similar. As a teacher who assumes authority, she initiates contact with the parents and as a caring and supportive teacher she makes them a part of what is going on in class by means of "parent-child activities" and by sending home "an information sheet for the parents, in Hebrew and Russian."

The aide is almost not present in the expected story except for her role in taking over the class for the teacher. The teacher leaves the aide in charge of the class, thus taking advantage of her as someone who can take over when necessary, freeing the teacher to do other things that are equally important.

Evaluation: Among the few means of evaluation used in the expected story are the following positive descriptions: "H, pleased with the attention I was giving her"; "The mother was satisfied with the individual attention she had been given"; "left . . . with a broad smile on her face".

Language: The story is marked by two primary semantic fields. One is happiness and satisfaction, and the other is empathy and support. The following expressions exemplify the semantic field of happiness and satisfaction: "pleased"; "I held H's hand, and together we went back to class". Examples from the field of empathy and support include: "I moved towards her to calm her down"; "I tried to be sympathetic"; "I understood"; " . . . she could come speak to me or to the mediator"; "I gave her the mediator's telephone number"; "I needed to give them a chance to openly and freely express their emotions and feelings"; "I wanted to restore their sense of security and to ensure them that I would always be there for them". Moreover, the text is marked by a cadence typical of fairy tales: "And so the three of us set off towards the teachers' room . . . "; "I held H's hand, and together we went back to class".

The teacher's sense of professional self emerges from the three components of the discourse analysis. This teacher sees herself as an authority figure whose role is to lead and to solve problems in the educational environment under her control (the classroom). Yet on the other hand she is also empathetic and caring, someone whose job it is to show sympathy and to guide those under her professional wing toward serenity and understanding.

The negligible use of evaluation devices in the expected story seems to indicate that the entire story is in line with the wishes of the teacher-narrator, so that such evaluations are unnecessary. Those means of evaluation that are used express feelings of happiness and satisfaction. Underlying the words is a fairytale-like tone emerging from the choice of expressions that sound as if taken from a fairy story with a happy ending. This choice signifies a reassuring and cheerful state of mind and a desire for everyone to live "happily ever after"—the teacher, her pupil, the pupil's mother, and the other children in the classroom and their parents.

The teacher-inquirer involved in the story describes how the process of self-study has contributed to her work as a teacher as follows. "The most significant contribution has been that I have acquired an essential tool that has made my educational practice more effective and will likely reduce professional burnout. The ability to analyze a personal professional incident, to understand what is implied in the incident, to discover that it is possible to act differently and to 'prevent the volcano from erupting' contributes to the peace of mind that we teachers need so badly."

In conclusion, in both the authentic and the expected cases of teaching the teacher positions herself as a figure of authority whose job it is to "educate." The difference in positioning is that in the first case, the authority figure of the teacher does not make any accommodations with respect to all the other characters involved, thus resulting in a direct confrontation with the mother, a feeling of disappointment in the aide's behavior and the need to involve a third party (the mediator) in order to solve her conflict with the mother. In the expected story, the teacher still expresses her position of authority as a professional educator, yet at the same time she is empathetic, understanding and supportive. The conflict is nipped in the bud, for the teacher is quick to solve the problem as best she can and out of her support and understanding for the "other." The language has a fairytale cadence and is sprinkled with expressions of satisfaction and happiness, empathy and support. In contrast to the many and varied evaluation devices in the authentic story, in this story the limited use of evaluations means conveys the teacher's sympathetic and supportive way of handling the incident as well as her satisfaction with how the incident was handled.

The story's title, "The "Promised" Land?" was not changed, for it is relevant both to the authentic and to the expected story. Nevertheless, in the expected story the title assumes a different meaning for it shows the cultural conflict in a different light. The question implied in the title is answered in the expected story. Cultural clashes can only be solved by understanding the other, by demonstrating empathy and by providing help while acting pleasantly, thus paving the way for newcomers to the "Promised Land."

Instructional Situation C: "I Always Want Eyes"[9]

The teacher-inquirers in this case aspired to describe a story of success because the pupil involved in the story changed, enabling him to realize his potential. The situation described here is not a one-time incident like those described in Cases A and B above, but rather the case of a pupil who developed and made progress over the entire school year thanks to what the teacher-inquirers considered the proper guidance of the teacher working with him. This is the story of a junior high school literature teacher who took it upon herself to focus on an individual pupil—Yossi[10]—who had been earmarked by the school as a poor pupil. This story came to this teacher's mind as soon as the instructional situations approach was presented in the M.Ed. class she was taking as part of her graduate studies. She understood that instructional situations analysis, which is based upon describing critical events, can be a useful tool for teachers. She immediately recognized that in this case the authentic story was the critical event and hence chose to tell a story of success. The authentic story describes a teacher's strategy for working with a pupil. This strategy was developed based on the teacher's insights gleaned through the lens of self-study. In effect, this authentic story is a form of research based on a previous action research, which took place throughout the school year. The expected story is a hypothetical story constructed by the teacher-inquirers and told from the point of view of another teacher who taught Yossi, the English teacher. That story was not considered a story of success, and the teacher-inquirers present it as the antithesis to the success in the authentic case.

Overall, instructional situation C differs from the previous two situations in a number of ways. First, it is a situation that developed over time rather than a one-time incident, as mentioned above. Second, it is a story of success defined as a critical event in the teacher's professional life. Third, the expected story is presented from the point of view of another teacher who was not successful in helping this poor pupil improve his studies.

Authentic Case of Teaching

"I Always Want Eyes"[11] – Nurturing Self-Efficacy[12] in a Poor Pupil

We have chosen to describe the teaching-learning process of a literature teacher teaching an eighth grader named Yossi (pseudonym). For both the teacher and for Yossi, branded by everyone as a poor pupil, this was a story of success in which Yossi made remarkable progress. This is a story every teacher can identify with because it is neither extreme nor unique.

Every morning Yossi, a fourteen-year-old boy, set out down the path to the junior high school, twenty minutes away from his home. When he reached the school's gate, he made a mad dash to his classroom, threw his schoolbag on his seat and headed for his friends, who usually were sitting on a bench outside the caretaker's office. Yossi liked his friends, but he didn't like studying and he really didn't like doing his homework. He often was "drawn in" to violent altercations and broke the school rules. His teachers considered him a poor pupil because of his lack of interest in his studies and his low achievements. In literature class he would sit at the front desk in the row to the right of the window, next to a girl who was extremely diligent and quiet. Even before the lesson began, he would place his notebook and book on the desk and stare directly at me, as if he had been waiting for this moment for a long time. Each time I went around checking homework, he would quietly and hesitantly say he had "forgotten" to do it. Yossi did not participate much in class discussions. He was quiet, and his achievements in literature were poor. His naïve and embarrassed looking eyes and his slightly unkempt appearance made me like him. More than once I found myself "rewarding" him with a playful pinch on the cheek or an affectionate expression such as "you're cute" or "sweetie," causing him to smile broadly but questioningly and to shut his eyes in embarrassment.

With time I learned from his parents and his homeroom teacher that I was Yossi's favorite teacher. This knowledge pleased me, but also made me wonder why he wasn't doing his homework and why his achievements in literature were so poor. One day I made up my mind that I wanted to help Yossi. I thought that by applying a structured program I could help him make progress.

Even though I had heard about Yossi's learning difficulties and behavioral problems, I felt I had limited information about him. I decided to get more information from his homeroom teacher. (I very much wanted to get to know him without any preconceived notions.) The homeroom teacher told me that Yossi had learning difficulties. She referred to him as a poor pupil, someone who was easily "dragged in" to things, and often involved in violent incidents during recess. According to her, he didn't study at all, and if he did any homework, he usually copied it. She also told me that in elementary school Yossi had been considered an excellent pupil, though he had received help for interpersonal communication problems.

I was unable to get what the homeroom teacher had said out of my mind. More than that, her report shed light on the gap between Yossi's behavior and progress in literature class and his described behavioral problems and failure to learn in his other classes. I spoke with Yossi after one of my classes and offered to help him. Yossi smiled, expressing his willingness with the word "yes" and with his eyes that seemed to sparkle with happiness.

We decided to meet on a regular basis, and Yossi told me what he expected from our meetings. He asked for help with homework, claiming that he did not know why he sometimes copied homework from others or didn't do his homework at all. During our regular discussions, his lack of motivation and unwillingness to do his homework became evident. At one of our meetings, I proposed checking Yossi's homework after each literature class and explaining the homework for the next lesson. After that, Yossi began doing his literature homework regularly.

As time went by, I became more and more ambivalent. On the one hand, Yossi was doing his homework regularly, was receiving my support and had begun to participate in class. On the other hand, I felt this was a superficial change resulting from Yossi's dependency on the help I was giving him. I decided to "study" Yossi in greater depth, and I began observing him in some other classes (English and Arabic). The Yossi I saw there was a different boy altogether. He copied his homework during the lesson, even though the teacher asked him not to. He acted like a "clown" and disrupted the class. After observing those classes, I understood Yossi was doing his literature homework to please me and that the problem had not been solved nor had there been any significant improvement.

Still, I was convinced that our deepening interpersonal relations based on mutual trust had led to his improved performance in literature class, as reflected in his homework and his class participation. I decided to consult the theoretical literature on the topic of homework. I was surprised to discover that the issue of homework was related to self-efficacy for learning. I did a lot of reading, and as I read one thing clearly emerged: Yossi and his behavior in all his classes, including his lack of motivation, problems with homework, sloppy and disorganized notebooks, tardiness problems, poor academic achievement and other issues as well.

I decided to formulate an overall strategic plan adapted to Yossi's world, needs and abilities. Yossi would implement this strategy in literature class and then apply it to his other classes. The strategy included the following: confronting the problem of homework and self-organized learning; planning a timetable for submitting literature assignments based on the pupil's own decisions; providing guidance in how to study for tests. After the strategy had been designed, our sessions were geared to achieving objectives and followed the following structure: setting a goal; making individual adaptations based upon learning strategies and the assignment topic; defining a task to achieve the projected goal, and providing feedback and reflection.

I was very pleased to see that this format for providing assistance and guidance helped motivate Yossi, as can be seen in the following:
- Yossi chose topics for submitting assignments: book reports, creative projects.
- Because we constructed the timetable for managing time together, Yossi submitted his assignments on time.
- Yossi continued to do his homework regularly and to organize his notebooks.
- Yossi and I also devised an appropriate test-taking strategy.
- In most of the sessions, we discussed his writing in his homework and book reports from the perspective of his ideas as well as his linguistic style, punctuation, etc.
- Yossi began to participate in class more and more.

Over time, my interpersonal relationship with Yossi intensified. His trust in me grew, and Yossi became more willing to learn and more interested in succeeding in literature classes. He spoke openly about his difficulties, his successes, his feelings and his desires. As a result of this process, Yossi began meeting deadlines we had set together and was personally complimented by significant adults around him (his homeroom teacher, the school principal and his parents) for his diligence and progress in literature. Moreover, his behavior in other classes and during recess improved as well, an improvement designated as "extremely successful."

On the last day of school, I called Yossi in for a talk. He came in with his report card in hand, opened it up and pointed excitedly to the word "literature." With a look of satisfaction and appreciation in his eyes, he ran his finger over what was written there: "80[13] – you take a serious interest in this subject." He shyly said, "This is the highest grade I've ever received except for gym class." His comment really touched me, engulfing me in a feeling of pain mixed with pleasure. I told Yossi I was proud of him and I loved him very much, and to show my appreciation I bought him two books. Yossi was very embarrassed. He didn't open the package, but he quickly read what I had written on the card.

Along with my words of appreciation was a quote from a poem by Darwin P. Kingsley which seemed to have been written especially for Yossi: "You have powers you never dreamed of. You can do things you never thought you could do. There are no limitations in what you can do except the limitations of your own mind. Don't think you cannot. Think you can."Although this learning process was cut short due to the end of the school year, it can still be seen as a quite satisfactory story of success. The most important thing is that Yossi believed he could achieve and succeed, and his thinking was changed by his success in literature. The school had considered him a poor pupil rather than one who lacked self-efficacy skills. This is a story of success mixed with feelings of having overlooked other children who go to school every day, those designated as poor pupils or under-achievers with limited abilities, whereas in reality all they are lacking is guidance, tools, strategies and a teacher willing to show them the way and help them realize their true abilities. The moral of this story is that we educators should always "want eyes" for our pupils, eyes sparkling with happiness.

Teacher-inquirers' interpretation. According to the teacher-inquirers, this case story includes several themes. Two tangential circles can be identified, each emerging from the other:

- The story of this particular teenage boy who symbolizes all children who are underachievers and are identified as poor pupils. With the proper learning strategies, these pupils can make substantial progress.
- The story of the literature teacher reporting this significant experience through which she "discovers" the pupil's abilities by researching her work, becoming familiar with the pupil's world, adapting strategies, and applying a consistent and methodical process involving feedback and reflection.

The teacher-inquirers position the teacher-narrator within the reality of subject-area teachers who teach in junior high school and have difficulty giving attention to each individual pupil. Another theme found in the story is self-efficacy and the teacher's role in directing the pupil toward such a learning strategy. Based upon the theoretical literature, the teacher-inquirers explain that first the teacher recognized there was a problem with the way the pupil was functioning. Gradually her acquaintance with the pupil deepened, and she began to focus on his difficulties and to understand his needs. The teacher-inquirers claim that the ongoing discussions with Yossi emphasizing his needs, difficulties and feelings constituted "a fundamental and significant component in the process of becoming acquainted with him." They further elaborate:

> The teacher began to see some progress in how the pupil prepared his homework for literature class, but he still was having difficulties and needed support (tardiness problems, disorganized notebooks, failure to turn in assignments on time and low test scores). This insight led her to consult the theoretical literature, where she discovered that Yossi's behavior and learning attributes were those of a pupil who lacks self-efficacy for learning.

The teacher-narrator's new insights regarding her role in guiding the learner toward learning strategies and in constructing a dialogue-based relationship with the learner led her to formulate a work plan with the pupil. The teacher-inquirers explain this as follows:

Based upon the teacher's understanding of the meaning of the dialectic between theory and practice, she formulated strategies that took both the literature curriculum and Yossi's individual needs into consideration. She also chose appropriate elements from the self-directed learning approach: study time management and submitting assignments on time, devising strategies to prepare for tests, writing improvement, selecting topics for assignments, and others as well. By allowing Yossi to choose the topics for his assignments, book reports and creative projects, she enabled him to grow and make progress. In effect, this freedom of choice generated interest and curiosity, and thus motivation.

According to the teacher-inquirers, this case provided the teacher an opportunity for significant learning based upon the dialectic between theory and practice. In effect, for the teacher-narrator this is a research study about research, or a meta-analysis. The case story is itself a story of research carried out by the teacher, motivated by her academic insights, through reading the research literature and through her ongoing interpretation of her own teaching in real time, as she develops her relationship with the learner. In practice this is an act of constructivist learning in the spirit of Vygotsky (1962). According to this approach, the act of teaching is within the learner's zone of proximal development, marking the difference between what a learner can do without help and what he or she can do with help. In fact it is "the distance between the actual developmental level as determined by independent problem solving and the level of potential development as determined through problem solving under adult guidance, or in collaboration with more capable peers" (Vygotsky, 1978, p. 86). Such development occurs through a process of dialogue between the teacher, who is the guiding adult, and the learner, who realizes his potential development (Ezer, 1998).

The two teacher-inquirers constructed another research activity in addition to the teacher's own in-action research, "analysis of the instructional situation," in that they pinpointed the central themes emerging from the case (the role of the subject-area teacher in directing a pupil identified as poor and in building a dialogical relationship with the pupil on a constructivist basis). Analyzing the case through the theoretical literature added another layer to their understanding of constructivist teaching and its contribution to the pupil's individual development and the teacher's professional development. They concluded their interpretive section with the following sentence: "The teacher had never had such an experience with an individual pupil during her entire teaching career, even though she had helped many pupils on an individual basis." This interpretation underlines their observation that self inquiry into an instructional situation is of great significance to the teacher-inquirer, marking a milestone in her professional development.

Expected case of teaching. In view of her own success and other teachers' lack of success in helping Yossi, the teacher-narrator decided to show the other side of the coin in the expected case: a subject-area teacher, in this case the English teacher, who did not follow the example of the literature teacher (the narrator) and did not apply self-study as a means for understanding and helping the pupil.

Story from the English Teacher's Perspective[14]

The story described in this case is neither exceptional nor isolated, and it can be handled in a number of ways. Therefore, we have chosen to tell a story that differs from the authentic case in that it is not a story of success. The story describes how a teacher handles a poor pupil in a way that does not change the boy and does not help him realize his potential. The story is told from the point of view of an English teacher who has been teaching for over twenty years. She teaches many classes and has numerous pupils. She must cope with the complexities of classroom management, find ways to integrate special needs pupils and still find time to teach the English curriculum. This teacher is not conversant with the development of new teaching-learning models and is not familiar with the theoretical literature on the topic of self-efficacy for learning.

The story goes like this . . .

Yossi, a fourteen-year-old boy, sat at the first desk in the second row to the right of the window. At the beginning of every English class, he diligently took out his notebook and book. Many times when I checked the homework and discovered he had not done his, Yossi would tell me he had "forgotten" to bring it. Yossi did not participate much in class. He was quiet during the lessons, and his achievements were quite poor. I decided to talk to the class homeroom teacher about Yossi to find out how he was doing in other classes and socially. The homeroom teacher told me about Yossi's learning and behavioral problems. She identified him as a poor pupil and as someone who was easily "drawn in" and therefore often involved in violence at recess. According to her, he did not study at all, and if he did hand in homework, he had copied it from someone else. She claimed he had been a very good pupil in elementary school, but now in junior high his achievements were low.

I found myself thinking that here's "another" pupil who doesn't devote any effort to his studies, and he seems to be "lazy" as well. I decided to have a talk with him during recess. I told him I saw he had not been studying and had no motivation or desire to do his homework. I pointed out that since he knew I recorded every time he did not hand in his homework, he should also be aware that his grade would be affected by this, which would be too bad for him. I attempted to encourage him to study and apply himself to his work. At the end of our discussion, Yossi said he would try to study and do his homework. In the subsequent classes I saw no change. Yossi continued to sit in class without participating, without showing any interest, and also without handing in his homework.

I thought it would be a good idea to speak with his parents. I would tell them that Yossi was not participating in my classes and ask them to talk with him and make sure he did his homework. That evening I called his house and spoke to his mother. I explained to her that pupils who did not apply themselves in English class developed gaps that were later very difficult to bridge, and that this situation was likely to have an impact on Yossi's achievements in this important subject in the future as well. For Yossi to make progress, he needed to do his homework on a regular basis, and it would be a good idea for him to get some help at home as well. Yossi's mother told me that she was aware that his situation at school was unsatisfactory and that he was busy with other things and did not devote time to his studies. She also understood the importance of English and had tried to talk with him, but so far she had not managed to make him study. She also began saying that she thought the teachers at school needed to "make some concessions" to Yossi by explaining the lessons to him on an individual basis. I told her I could speak only for myself, explaining I had lots of pupils and was doing my utmost during class to explain the material in a way everyone could understand. I also reviewed the material, checked the homework in class, and explained what was unclear to those who tried to understand. The mother asked me to speak with Yossi and try to help him. I told her I had already spoken with him and that I would do so again, and she promised to try to encourage him to study. After my talk with Yossi's mother, I was left with the feeling that she was trying to divert responsibility from the home and the boy and that in effect she could not cope with her son. I also thought that expecting us to give her son individual attention was out of line. How could we do this when there were so many pupils? Parents must see to it that their child studied at school, and if he was having difficulties, they needed to have these difficulties evaluated and get him some help. Yossi did not study in his other classes as well, and he also had behavioral problems that needed to be dealt with. In thinking about my work, I told myself I devoted great efforts to prepare the lessons well and give the pupils as much individual attention as possible. If pupils were lazy, I could not force them to learn. I was doing my best under the circumstances.

A few days later, I tried talking to Yossi again at recess, but he apparently was busy and tried to avoid me. I decided to talk with the homeroom teacher again to see if she could help. She told me that many teachers had complained that Yossi was not studying and was continuing to behave violently. To my regret, at the end of the school year Yossi still had not changed his ways. I felt I had somehow missed an opportunity, and thought that perhaps I should have consulted the theoretical literature to see what was new in coping with poor pupils. Maybe there was some way to reach them and make things easier for them.

What stands out in this expected story is the English teacher's good intentions with respect to teaching Yossi and helping him do better in English. But also quite apparent are the teacher's feelings of helplessness. She feels that professionally she has done her utmost: she spoke to the pupil, gave him short-term assignments, spoke to his parents, and involved others at the school such as the homeroom teacher. Yet despite all her efforts, and because he is not the only pupil in the class, she is powerless to help this specific boy, leaving her at the end of the year with a feeling of having "missed an opportunity."

Clearly the teacher-inquirers, who are telling this hypothetical story through the eyes of another subject-area teacher, are attempting to paint a picture that is common in the educational system: a teacher who makes every effort to reach every pupil, but fails due to objective conditions such as large classes and lack of parental cooperation, thus suffering professional disappointment.

Sense of professional self emerging from the cases. In this section, discourse analysis is applied to the manner in which the stories were told in order to reveal the sense of professional self of the teacher involved in each case. As in instructional situations A and B, here too each story is analyzed, according to the three components of discourse analysis: positioning, evaluation and use of language.

Critical discourse analysis of authentic case of teaching. The opening of the story is placed in a dual context. The first context is that of the factors and deliberations involved in selecting the case. The second context describes Yossi: his age, his situation in school before entering the teacher-narrator's literature class, and his usual behavior in the classroom. The story goes on to focus on the relationship between the teacher and Yossi, and on the strategy she adopted in working with him. Concurrently, the story also focuses on the teacher herself: her thoughts, her insights as time goes by and the things she takes into consideration in teaching Yossi. The story's coda again brings up the teacher-narrator's reflections as she thinks about how this story of success can be generalized to apply to all educators. The use of the figure of speech "I always want eyes" as the title of the story and at the end of the story points to the teacher-narrator's focus on her sense of professional self. The relationship or dialogue between teacher and pupil was initiated and built by the teacher herself. "I" am the one who wants the pupil's eyes; the direction is from the initiating teacher to the pupil, who responds to her initiative. The "eyes" symbolize listening, attentiveness and also counseling. The pupil pays attention and listens, and acts according to the teacher's counsel. That is, the teacher initiates, and she is responsible and accountable for the pupil under her care.

The title of the story is taken from a poem by Natan Zach[15]: "I always want eyes to see the beauty in the world and to praise this wonderful and impeccable beauty . . . ." The positive connotation of this allusion illuminates how beautiful and praiseworthy this story of success is in the eyes of the teacher-narrator.

Positioning: The teacher-narrator positions herself in the authentic case story mainly with respect to the pupil. As indicated above, this positioning begins with the story's title, and it is one-directional: she is the initiator, the one who "wants eyes," which she metaphorically receives as a result of her self-initiated acts. These are acts of love ("More than once I found myself 'rewarding' him with a playful pinch on the cheek or an affectionate expression") and acts of support ("I spoke with Yossi . . . and offered to help him"; "I proposed . . . "). It can be assumed that her responses were the opposite of those he was accustomed to getting in school and constituted the basis for their ongoing work together. At first, the teacher led and the pupil followed, a positioning the teacher clearly understood: "I understood that Yossi was doing his literature homework to please me . . . ." Nevertheless, the teacher was "convinced that our deepening interpersonal relations [were] based on mutual trust." As the story progresses, the positioning remained as it was. The teacher is the initiator, formulating work strategies with Yossi to increase his motivation to study, and the pupil responds to these initiatives. The teacher interprets this as "deepening interpersonal relations based on mutual trust." Still, Yossi remains a "pupil" responding to the teacher's initiatives even when he begins achieving: "Yossi began meeting deadlines we had set together . . . his behavior in other classes and during recess improved as well . . . ." He showed respect for the teacher out of a desire to please her. He was embarrassed and bashful when he showed his achievements to the teacher. At the end of the story, the teacher still sees herself as the initiator in their relationship, and as a sign of her appreciation for his response to their work strategies and his good academic achievements, she rewards the pupil with books and words of appreciation.

The story also includes another positioning, that of the teacher vis-à-vis her colleagues, the other subject-area teachers. She positions herself as part of this community of teachers. This positioning provides the general context for the story, and thus appears at the beginning and at the end. The following framing statement appears in the story's introduction: "This is a story every teacher can identify with because it is neither extreme nor unique." The story ends with the following sentence: "The moral of this story is that we educators should always 'want eyes' . . . ." This sentence again positions the teacher within the community of teachers where she feels she belongs.

Evaluation: The story includes several means of evaluation, both those of the teacher-narrators together in the first part narrated in the first person plural, and those of the teacher involved in the described instructional case in the part narrated in the first person singular. At the beginning, the two teacher-inquirers make an explicit statement of evaluation in which they specifically claim that every teacher can identify with this story: "This is a story every teacher can identify with." Toward the end of the story, the two teacher-inquirers make another such explicit statement in which they directly point to the story as a story of success: "Although this learning process was cut short due to the end of the school year, it can still be seen as a quite satisfactory story of success."

The teacher-narrator presents her point of view through a number of descriptions, as follows: The pupil "*made a mad dash* to his classroom . . . "; "next to a girl who was *extremely diligent and quiet*"; he spoke to the teacher "*hesitantly*". Other major means of evaluation in the story include the use of quotation marks to indicate irony or for emphasis. Irony can be seen in such expressions as "He often was '*drawn in* '"; "he would quietly and hesitantly say he had '*forgotten*' to do it [his homework]"; "More than once I found myself '*rewarding*' him with a playful pinch on the cheek or an affectionate expression . . . ." The emphasis is used to express the opposite of what ostensibly seems to be. Some examples are "a '*poor*' pupil"; "a

'*superficial* change"; "I decided to '*study*' Yossi in greater depth";
"I saw . . . '*a different boy*'_altogether"; "He acted like a '*clown*'." Other
than these, there are very few expressions of evaluation in the teacher-
narrator's story.

Language: The story begins in the first person plural ("We have chosen
to describe"), continues in the third person ("For both the teacher and for
Yossi . . . this was a success story"), and then moves to the first person
singular, the voice of the teacher-narrator ("His naïve and embarrassed
looking eyes . . . made *me* . . . *I* found myself . . . . With time *I* learned . . .").
The last line of the story returns to the first person plural: "*we* educators
should always . . . ."

The most recurrent semantic field refers to reflections and decision-
making, as seen in the verbs used by the teacher-narrator:

"This knowledge pleased me, but also caused me to *wonder* . . . "

"I *thought* that by beginning . . . I could help him progress."

"I *felt* I had limited information about him. I *decided to get more
information* . . . "

"I *decided to* '*study*' Yossi in greater depth . . . "

"I *decided to consult* the theoretical literature . . . "

"I *felt* this was an 'artificial' change . . . "

"I *discovered* that the issue of homework was related to . . . "

"I *decided to formulate* an overall strategic plan . . . "

The teacher-narrator's relationship with the pupil is marked by verbs of
support and assistance sprinkled with fondness: "I found myself '*rewarding*'
him . . . "; "I *spoke with* Yossi . . . and *offered* to help him"; "I *proposed*
checking Yossi's homework after each literature class and *explaining* the
homework for the next lesson . . . ."

In general, the sense of professional self of the teacher leading this
instructional situation emerges from her position of someone in authority.
The decisions she makes about the pupil are based upon her professional
judgment after having "studied" the object of her teaching (the pupil). The
evaluation devices reveal her perception of the instructional situation as a
story of success from which other teachers can also learn. Her sense of
professional self is of a practical-reflective teacher confidently guiding her
pupils toward achievement based upon her self-study and her ongoing and
constructive relationship with the pupil, which she herself built through
heightened and individual attention to the pupil, affection, and formulation

of a learning strategy. In her view, the very fact that she is a practical and reflective teacher who uses academic means ("studying the topic") to structure her knowledge about her pupils and her pupils' knowledge as well is in itself a professional success story. The shift from first person plural to third person to first person singular indicates the teacher-inquirers have begun to comprehend their position as teachers within a professional community. It also shows that they understand their story is indeed neither extreme nor unique and can be successfully applied by their colleagues.

Critical discourse analysis of expected case of teaching. A different sense of professional self emerges from the expected story, which is ostensibly told by another subject-area teacher who acted "differently" and not in a practical-reflective manner. This teacher makes every effort to teach the boy who is having difficulty, but despite her efforts she fails. Overall, she strongly believes that the subject she teaches is important and hence every pupil must learn it. The expected story also provides two contexts at the beginning. The general context for the story is the story of the English teacher, which according to the teacher-inquirers "is neither exceptional nor isolated" but is also "not a success story." The other context is the specific teaching context: the teacher, her years of teaching experience, her current knowledge of innovative teaching methods, etc. The story's coda guides the teacher-narrator toward a change in her perception of her professional self: "Perhaps I should have consulted the theoretical literature to see what was new in coping with poor pupils." At this point, the expected story is linked to the authentic story, with a hint that if the English teacher had followed the example of the literature teacher, her teaching story would have been a story of success as well.

Positioning: The teacher-narrator positions herself with respect to a number of characters in the story: the pupil, the homeroom teacher and the parents. In addition, she positions herself within the community of subject-area teachers. Unlike the literature teacher from the authentic story, the English teacher seeks partners.

With respect to the pupil, the teacher positions herself as an authority figure whose job it is to determine the course of the lesson. She is the type of teacher who gives orders to the pupil: "I told him I saw he was not studying and had no motivation . . . ." For his part, the pupil does not follow the teacher's instructions: ". . . he apparently was busy and tried to avoid me." Therefore, according to her, "Yossi still had not changed his ways." This is because the teacher-narrator sees him as "another pupil who does not devote any effort to his studies, and he seems to be lazy as well." Their relationship is between an authority figure who wants to give (the teacher) and an evasive, unmotivated character who does not want to receive (the pupil).

With respect to the homeroom teacher, the teacher positions herself as a colleague interacting with another colleague, or to be more precise, as part of the professional context. Both are disturbed by the "situation of the pupils" in their role as teachers, and they consider themselves equals among equals within the professional community. Their relationship is businesslike, matter of fact, untarnished: "I decided to talk to the class homeroom teacher about Yossi to get some information about how he was doing . . . ."; "She told me that many teachers have complained . . . ."

With respect to the mother, the teacher positions herself as an authority figure who knows her profession and therefore has the authority to give instructions to the parents: "I explained to her [the mother] that . . . it would be a good idea for him to get some help at home . . . I told her . . . ." The mother does not accept the teacher's authority, and indeed accuses the educational system and expects the teacher to do all the teaching work: "She [the mother] also began saying that she thought the teachers at school needed to 'make some concessions' to Yossi by explaining the lessons to him on an individual basis"; "The mother asked me to talk to Yossi and try to help him . . . ." As in the relationship with the pupil, here too there is an authority figure who knows her job (the teacher), and a figure who does not accept her authority and expects her to act on her own in the teaching context (the mother). The authority figure of the teacher also contains a self-defensive tone, as seen in the following:

> I told her . . . I had lots of pupils and was doing my utmost during class to explain the material in a way everyone could understand. I also reviewed the material, checked the homework in class, and explained what was unclear to those who tried to understand.

Evaluation: The teacher uses explicit means of evaluation to interpret the reality of her work: "I attempted to encourage him to study and apply himself to his work"; "In thinking about my work, I told myself I devoted great efforts to prepare the lessons well and to give the pupils as much individual attention as possible. If pupils were lazy, I could not force them to learn. I was doing my best under the circumstances." She also expresses explicit judgment on how the pupil's parents respond: "I was left with the feeling that she [the mother] was trying to divert the responsibility from the home and the boy and that in effect she could not cope with her son. I also thought that expecting us to give her son individual attention was out of line."

In a few isolated cases, the teacher uses judgmental adjectives: the pupil is "lazy" while the subject she teaches is "important." The expected story also uses quotation marks to indicate irony and emphasis. Their ironic use is found at the beginning of the story, when the teacher describes the pupil's general behavior: "Yossi would tell me he had *'forgotten'* to bring it [his homework]." The quotation marks are used primarily for emphasis. Contrary to the emphasis in the authentic story, here the emphasis is for purposes of labeling and generalization. For example, the teacher-narrator refers to Yossi as *"another"* pupil who doesn't devote any effort to his studies, and he seems to be *"lazy"* as well. Yossi's mother claims that the school should *"make some concessions"* to Yossi. In one case, a parenthetical expression is used to describe the pupil's failure to change despite the teacher's great efforts: *"To my regret,* at the end of the school year Yossi still had not changed his ways." While this expression openly refers to the teacher's "regret," it also implies that this "regret" does not stem from her failure to help the pupil but rather from the failure of others involved in the story (the pupil himself, the parents, the homeroom teacher).

Language: The language used in the expected story is quite similar to that in the authentic story. Here, too, the story begins in the first person plural of the teacher-inquirers: ". . . we have chosen to tell a story that differs . . . ." The story then moves into the third person singular, referring to the English teacher: "The story is told from the point of view of an English teacher . . . ." The main story is told by the English teacher in the first person singular.

The most recurrent semantic field is the field of self-thinking and decision-making: "I found myself thinking"; "I decided to have a talk with him"; "In thinking about my work, I told myself . . . ." Another semantic field is that of statements with implied commands: "I pointed out that he [the pupil] should be aware . . . ."; "I explained to her [the mother] that pupils who did not apply themselves . . . developed gaps . . . "; "I told her [the mother] . . . ." Some of the statements are softened by a complex syntactical predicate: "I attempted to encourage him to study and apply himself to his work"; "I thought it would be a good idea to speak with . . ."; "it would be a good idea for him to get some help." This type of language indicates that the teacher assumes her behavior reflects her investment of time and resources, for she "attempted" and she suggested "it would be a good idea . . . ."

In summary, the expected story is ostensibly presented through the eyes of the English teacher, but in effect it is being told by the teacher-narrators, who probably find it difficult to step out of their professional frame of reference and their educational world view. Therefore, its discourse is quite similar to that of the authentic story. In both stories the teacher is the central figure, and the positioning is primarily vis-à-vis the pupil, though new characters are added and positioned in the expected story.

Each of the stories reveals a clear and solid sense of professional self for the subject-area teacher. The positioning, the use of evaluation devices and the language used by the teacher-narrator in each of the stories work together to suggest that the teacher cannot count on outsiders to help in nurturing and advancing the poor pupil. She can rely only on herself. Because all of her efforts were unsuccessful, apparently she needs to act differently, "academically," as seen in the last sentence of the expected story: " . . . perhaps I should have consulted the theoretical literature to see what was new in coping with poor pupils." Because the expected story is told from the perspective of the teacher-inquirers, it is constructed in a didactic fashion. It takes into consideration the community of subject-area teachers who are making every effort within the confines of their jobs to teach their pupils and to cope with poor pupils, yet their efforts are in vain. The story's didactic approach is expressed in the lesson to be learned from it. This strategy is implemented by leading up to the story's climax: the teacher's epiphany that it is better not to depend upon others and her sense of her practical-reflective professional self. That is, she sees herself as a teacher who must examine her own teaching environment, learn about it and act according to the conclusions she reached from her academic study of the theoretical literature.

In conclusion, the two stories—the authentic and the expected story— lead up to this same conclusion, and reveal the sense of professional self of the two teacher-inquirers who wrote these stories.

The Significance of Analyzing Instructional Situations for Teacher-Inquirers

The three instructional situations presented in this chapter guided the teacher-inquirers to new insights based on identifying the themes in the stories and reading the relevant theoretical literature. Each case led the teacher-inquirers to write an alternative story—the expected story—be it a success story due to "more correct" conduct based upon interpretation of the theoretical literature, or a story of lack of success, again based on insights from the theoretical literature. Instructional situation C, a case story constituting a research study about research, more clearly demonstrates the significance of research as a tool for teachers in their practical work. In the described case, reflecting about the research is what generated the practical-reflective perspective in which the case story is set.

The discourse analysis of the authentic and expected stories revealed each teacher-narrator's sense of professional self, which varied from teacher to teacher and therefore can be said to depend upon context and narrator.

Beyond its role in identifying the teacher-narrators' sense of professional self, research on the topic of instructional situations analysis made an additional impression upon the teacher-inquirers. Following are some of the teacher-inquirers' comments during the inquiry and after it as well. These statements clearly express the significance of research into instructional situations analysis for the teacher-inquirers:

> During my years working in education, I have encountered many situations and had many experiences with teachers, parents and teachers that were not so easy for me. I never stopped to think about . . . what was and what could have been . . . I just 'went with the flow,' like all my teacher colleagues, I learned to survive using the few tools at my disposal . . . .

> Writing up the case helped me understand what I go through 'in the heat of the moment' . . . while on the job . . . it brought me new insights that will help me act differently now and in the future.

Other comments referred to the meaning of "stopping and taking a step back" from the rat race of teaching and its superficial opportunities for examination and reflection:

> For me as a teacher, writing up the case was like looking into a mirror reflecting my everyday work behavior. Putting the case into words enabled me to take a momentary break from the rat race of working at school and to look differently and more intensely, from a different perspective even, at my responses as a teacher and at my behavior in the specific case.

The following testifies to the complexity of the case the teacher investigated:

> Writing up the case provided me with a tool to reflect upon my work in the classroom. Through writing up the case, I managed to understand that the case I chose to present was extremely complex. As a teacher, I tried to understand my alternatives in that case and how I had ultimately coped with it. In addition, I learned about myself as a professional, about my weaknesses and my strengths. I learned how I act in my work environment and why I act that way. In other words, I learned what motivates me to act and work in the classes I teach.

The research process enabled the teacher to understand the critical nature of the event, not merely to sense it. According to one of the teacher-inquirers, the research made it possible to "create a sense of detachment and to investigate the events . . . to enter the depths of the soul (which is impossible in everyday reality) and to shed light on the problem, the difficulty, the success." Moreover, the teacher-inquirers began to understand the significance of disseminating their new knowledge among their teacher colleagues. "The instructional situation is a means for publicizing the individual stories of teachers, who are usually alone, flying solo so to speak, and for distributing them to the entire sector." As one of the participants noted, research is seen as a "safe space" that "facilitates observation which is nearly objective, without any of the emotional baggage I was entangled with during the incident itself. The degree of emotion is not any less sharp, but it is more under control and can be observed from a certain distance."

The teacher-inquirers also evaluated the meaning of writing up the cases:

> The writing, or more precisely the writing process or the written event, enabled me as a teacher to hold a dialogue with my past experiences, with discussions I had held, with my own experiences and those of my colleagues. Writing gave me the opportunity for a dialogue with myself and with my past in a possible attempt to build something different in the future, indeed to build the future. I can metaphorically look at the writing process as a channel—this channel is the present, it contains the past and it faces the future.

This teacher-inquirer has chosen an interesting metaphor: writing is a *channel* that constitutes the present, contains the past and faces the future. Thus the teacher hints at the continuity of her work based upon new insights and future renewal. It is interesting to point to some other metaphors used by the teacher-inquirers in the above statements to describe self-study and the act of writing:

"For me as a teacher, writing up the case was like *looking in a mirror reflecting* my everyday work behavior." Writing was also seen as providing the teacher an opportunity for "a dialogue with myself and with my past." Other metaphors referred to the research act itself, which was seen as a "*safe space.*" Research helped the teacher understand "what I go through '*in the heat of the moment*'." Research enabled another teacher to "take a momentary break in the *rat race* of working at school." Through research, teacher-inquirers can "*prevent the volcano from erupting*" and help them achieve "*peace of mind.*"

These metaphors indicate that teachers gain meaning from self-study through analysis of instructional situations by building a collage to reflect this meaning. This type of research creates a safe space that allows dialogue with the self and the past by looking into the mirror to understand what is actually going on, while taking a break from the rat race of work, in order to prevent the volcano from erupting and to achieve the peace of mind teachers are so badly in need of.

For the teacher-inquirer, then, research is "an essential tool that has made educational work more effective and will likely reduce professional burnout."

CRITICAL AUTOBIOGRAPHY

Critical autobiography is made up of cases that constitute the building blocks of one's life story. As such, critical autobiography can help teachers understand their professional choices and the essence of what it means to be a teacher today. Critical autobiographical writing rests on two concepts: the prefix auto-, meaning "of the self," and *biography*. Recently this type of writing has come to represent one of the ways individuals can tell their personal or professional stories (Harris, 2005). In the context of the teaching profession, critical autobiography is in effect a form of self-narrative research in which teacher-inquirers link their personal experiences to their pedagogical beliefs and to the their professional theoretical context. Numerous disciplines engage in research and dialogue pertaining to narrative and autobiography. This research form is at the core of feminist research. It also derives from the oppressive ideologies (Sharkey, 2004), for it enables voices that until now were practically never heard at all to be heard loudly and clearly, not only as narratives but also on the critical level. Because autobiography is a form of narrative research, it clearly constitutes important evidence in documenting a life. At the same time, it is also a work of art akin to a literary creation (Freeman, 2007). Bamberg (2006) sees autobiography as narrative. He asserts that autobiography consists of unmediated memories told from the writer's perspective. Therefore, in his view, the emphasis in reading autobiography is on empathy, rather than on the desire to become enlightened, as guiding the reading/listening process. This is a narratology approach, which is backward-oriented.

In critical autobiographical writing, writers undergo a process that emerges from their own background. This genre allows writers to achieve closure, for not only does it enable them and their reference group—that is, the professional community in which they operate—to become better acquainted with one another, it also helps them better understand each other and the environmental influences on their own development (Benesch, 1993). The approach is based upon Freire's (1996) notion that writing is an act of liberation. Writing enables writers to become aware of their place in the world vis-à-vis that of others, and eventually to confront their thoughts, feelings, attitudes, and value system with those of others, whether the prevailing views or those of other minority groups. Not only does critical autobiography help writers answer major questions in their fields of interest, it also helps them examine their own values as they change over time (Clements, 1999). In autobiographical writing, the writers refer to forces that have affected them and scrutinize their own history over time in light of their cultural values and those of other cultural groups. This process enables the writers to think about their own lives and construct a positive identity (Harris, 2005).

Critical autobiography obviously differs from writer to writer in its presentation and its focus. As noted, critical autobiography is a form of self-study through which researchers are transformed into active interpreters of the past with the goal of understanding and effectively applying their abilities and interests in the present and the future. The writing is based upon personal memories (Robinson & Taylor, 1998; Bamberg, 2006). These memories represent "the truth" at a particular time as seen through the eyes of the writer. When it becomes a systematic examination of the writer's own biography or life history within the social, cultural and political context, critical autobiography becomes a research tool. Nevertheless, we must keep in mind that memory is fictive. That is, what we believe to be the truth, even if it is in fact incorrect, is the product of our perspectives and interpretations over time and has validity (Clements, 1999). Robinson and Taylor (1998) distinguish between autobiographical memory, defined as a collection of disorganized short-term and long-term memories, and self-narrative, which is a more "narrative" and organized representation of the self. According to Robinson and Taylor, because people remember different things—some more important and some less—not all the events included in an auto-biography are relevant to research. The narrative itself, in contrast, is organized in chronological order and includes events revolving around clear themes. Despite this, they believe that autobiographies and self-narratives do not document life. Rather, they are versions of life comprising cultural forms that represent what the narrators believe to be life.

In this book I regard autobiography as self-narrative organized around themes related to the lives of teachers and the professional impact of anecdotes from their lives on their work and identity. This chapter uses the term "critical autobiography" to refer to a description of individual memories seen through the lens of personal experience, reflection and rethinking and linked to prevailing sociopolitical contexts and perspectives (Ezer, 2004). In practice, not only does autobiographical writing facilitate examining history from an individual perspective that takes into account political incidents, professional occurrences, academic experience and other life events, but it also makes it possible to revisit these periods and events from a more distant perspective (Harris, 2005). Language plays a major role in this reflection and rethinking, for the ways in which we designate objects and abstract terms and describe our experiences are the ways in which we preserve social power patterns (Sharkey, 2004). Hence, an outside reader can use critical discourse analysis to examine various aspects of critical autobiography and to consider not only "what" the narrators said but "how" they said it.

Over the years, teachers have written about their work in teaching and about what led them to the teaching profession. We may then pose this question: Does writing about teaching make a teacher a better teacher? Let us assume that we all believe teachers in the school system should be "good teachers." But what constitutes a good teacher? Policymakers in Israel have led us to believe that "a good teacher is a teacher for life," though very few "good" teachers have told their stories from the "inside," out of their authentic experience in teaching. Most well known are internationally published books, such as *Teacher* by Sylvia Ashton-Warner, first published in 1963. Another such book is *Teacher Man* by Frank McCourt, published in 2005.

In *Teacher*[16], Ashton-Warner describes her exceptional teaching techniques, in particular her revolutionary method for teaching reading. The book is written in the first person and is unique in that it is based upon the writer's professional experience. The book tells the teacher's story, but also includes a collection of the pupils' stories from the classroom. The teacher's story is peppered with the writer's thoughts and worldviews, as in the following: "First words must have intense meaning for a child. They must be part of his being" (p. 33). She also writes about herself. "I never teach a child something and then get him to write about it" (p. 54). Some of her examples from the classroom are descriptive, as in "Ten o'clock is backache time. By then you have spent a half hour bending over the children writing at their low desks . . . ." (p. 55). Others are in dialogue form.

> Later, standing watching Seven grinding his chalk to dust on his blackboard as usual . . . I do see. 'Whom do you want, Seven? Your old Mummy or your new Mummy?' 'My old Mummy.' 'What do your brothers do?' 'They all hits[17] me' (p. 37).

The author's reflections emerge from statements like the following: "You never want to say that it's good or bad. That's got nothing to do with it. You've got no right at all to criticise the content of another's mind. A child doesn't make up his own mind. It's just there . . ." (pp. 57–58). Ashton-Warner often presents the teaching case together with her own worldviews, as in the following:

> I think that the educational story from the infant room to the university is like the writing of a novel. You can't be sure of your beginning until you have checked it with your ending. What might come of infant teachers visiting the university and professors visiting the infant room? I had two other professors in my infant room last year and they proved themselves not only to be delightfully in tune but sensitively helpful. Yet what I believe and what I practice are not wholly the same thing" (p. 98).

Throughout the book, Ashton-Warner interweaves descriptions of instructional situations with her professional philosophy of life and reflective musings on what she has experienced.

McCourt (2005) takes a different approach in his book. He moves back and forth between the personal and the professional, describing his professional development in the form of a saga based upon his childhood and his immigration from Ireland to the United States. The book opens on a personal note, looking back on his past. "If I knew anything about Sigmund Freud and psychoanalysis I'd be able to trace all my troubles to my miserable childhood in Ireland"[18]. He continues to the present, assessing his profession at the time of writing the book: "How I became a teacher at all and remained one is a miracle and I have to give myself full marks for surviving all those years in the classrooms of New York."

As teachers, we find it interesting to read about the lives of other teachers. Suddenly our profession takes on a radiance we never attributed to it. Suddenly what goes on in our little sphere of influence is happening, albeit somewhat differently, to someone else on the other side of the world. Suddenly our profession seems interesting, even if the author of the book declares that "there was nothing remarkable about my thirty years in the high school classrooms of New York City" (p. 11). Nothing may have been remarkable to McCourt, but what happened to him provided material for a book of almost 300 pages. Apparently everything happens, even when nothing remarkable happens. As someone who works in the field of literacy, I cannot help but note here that this is an example of the power of literacy in connecting people from around the world, in linking brains from different cultures, and most importantly, in developing critical thinking to enable us to see ourselves and our lives within the context of other lives. Readers, and particularly those from the field described in the book, are interested in the experiences of others. Perhaps we can learn about our own experiences in the field, and perhaps we can learn that we are not alone in our work experiences.

Many films have also depicted the stories of teachers coping with problematic classes. *To Sir, with Love, Stand and Deliver,* and *Dead Poets Society* are among the films portraying teachers, their teaching dilemmas and their solutions for problematic instructional situations they faced. These films depict the stories of teachers who, despite adversity, achieved professional success.

The stories of teachers we have read or seen in movies were those of "other teachers," sometimes told through the eyes of outsiders who projected their own interpretations on the teachers' stories, and sometimes through the eyes of the teachers themselves. Such stories appear in academic works edited by researchers and theoreticians, for example, *Stories from the Heart* by Meyer (1996) or *Stories Teachers Tell,* edited by Hartman (1998), which reflects on literacy in teachers' professional practice. Narrative inquiry in the form of teachers' self-study has also not been overlooked and is described in depth in a book edited by Kubler LaBoskey (2002), for example.

Nonetheless, when reading someone else's story, readers will always position themselves with respect to the other storyteller. As opposed to the narratives of others, in critical autobiographies individuals can position themselves with respect to themselves and critique the events of their lives from afar, from the academic perspective of researchers and theoreticians. This quality differentiates critical autobiography from McCourt's book, for example, in which the author compares his professional and personal life "back then" with what he thinks now, in his sixties, and with what has often been reported in the literature which he frequently quotes as a former language arts teacher. Critical autobiography is a further step in the professional life of an individual. It is more than merely autobiography with a critical point of view, the product of an individual's maturity at the time the story is being told. Rather, it is autobiography attempting to explain itself not only from the perspective of the individual telling the story, but also from the points of view of other academic scholars as interpreted by the story's narrator.

We have not heard enough of the authentic voices of teachers telling their stories systematically and thoughtfully, safely distanced by time from the events described. We have not heard enough about teachers transforming a research tool into a tool for analyzing their life stories and reaching new insights to help them develop professionally. We have not heard enough about critical autobiography as a meaningful tool in teachers' professional development. This chapter, then, is dedicated first and foremost to describing these teachers who have established their professional identities using critical autobiography. Later I point out the significance of this unique form of self-study.

Over the years, critical autobiography has developed as part of the post-modernist multicultural approach. It is a tool that enables the "other," whoever he or she may be, to make his or her voice heard and to achieve an understanding about his or her identity and position in the personal, social and professional world in which he or she lives (Ezer, 2004). This approach sees writing as an expression of liberation (Freire, in Shor & Freire, 1987). It stresses that this form of writing

> "…enables writers to make themselves conscious of their situation in the world in view of the situation of others, and ultimately to confront their thoughts, feelings, attitudes, and value systems with those of others in dominant or minority groups (Ezer, 2004, p. 61).

Indeed, writing critical autobiography serves as a means of emancipation and a way toward achieving multicultural literacy.

In addition to discussing the above attributes of critical autobiography, this chapter also emphasizes the role of this form of writing as a self-study tool used by teachers to achieve professional empowerment that may ultimately lead to significant professional development. During the course of my work as a lecturer at a teacher education college, I have integrated critical autobiography as a research tool in a seminar I taught on Multiculturalism and Multilingualism. Some of my graduate students, also experienced teachers who went back to school for an M.Ed. degree, took up this challenge and chose to use this research method in their seminar work. For the most part these were students who had something to say about their personal and social situation, and accordingly aimed their research toward the multicultural context. One student, for example, a divorcee, chose to examine what in her life had brought her to her current state, and what it meant to her to be a young divorced woman within Israeli society. Another student examined her immigration from an English-speaking country to Israel, while still another looked at her "life's journey" as an Israeli woman who had spent most of her adult life studying at international institutions outside of Israel. Still others investigated their personal histories as part of a group: growing up in a particular ethnic group and the intercultural conflicts they experienced in Israel, a country that welcomes immigration. Only a few chose to examine their autobiographies in the context of their work as teachers—that is, how critical events in their lives were related to their essence as teachers, or what in their personalities had led them to choose the teaching profession.

One such story is that of Idit, an elementary school teacher with twenty years of experience teaching first through fifth grades. Her story is presented in the following section as an example of critical autobiography focusing on critical events that led the teacher to choose the teaching profession. Idit undertook her self-study with the following questions: *Why am I a teacher in spite of and regardless of everything, and what kind of teacher am I?* Galit's story, the second study presented in the chapter, is also a critical autobiographical self-study. Galit examines her early childhood and how it affected the person she has become—a woman, a mother, a professional teacher, a school principal and a counselor. Galit's questions in undertaking this self-study were: *How did my childhood shape my adult persona today, and how have the passages in my life affected who I am today?*

I have chosen these two stories as examples of critical autobiographical self-study because each relates to the teacher as a researcher, and each, in its own way, clarifies why the teacher-inquirer has become what she is today. Both stories grew out of baggage each teacher brought from her past, a burden each sought to clarify and understand as a mature adult with many years of teaching experience. Each teacher became a stronger individual by her research. One was fortified by finally understanding why she is a teacher "in spite of and regardless of everything," as manifested by the title she gave her work after it was completed. The second was strengthened by her decision to forgive and made even stronger by the most meaningful decision of her life—to slow down her race for career advancement, to be first of all a woman and a mother and only then a teacher and counselor.

IDIT'S CRITICAL AUTOBIOGRAPHY: "IN SPITE OF AND REGARDLESS OF EVERYTHING—A TEACHER" [19]

Idit, a graduate student, chose to examine the events of her life story and their impact on her professional work. Over the course of an entire year, she carried out a self-study which examined why she chose the teaching profession and what led her to be the teacher she is today. Through Idit's work I demonstrate the process of writing critical autobiography, as well as the reciprocal relations between her as teacher-inquirer-writer and me as her thesis advisor. I also discuss the significance of critical autobiography in the teacher-inquirer's personal and professional development.

Idit's work emerged from a statement she made to me at the beginning of her master's degree studies.

When I was in first grade, I knew I wanted to be a teacher, despite my teacher at the time who did everything she could to hamper my progress. I knew I wanted to be a 'different' kind of teacher when I grew up, not like her.

This sentence provided the motivation for her self-study. My spontaneous response was as follows. "Why don't you try to examine what led up to your being a teacher today, and how your past experiences can shed light on what is going on today, that is on how you conduct yourself in your teaching." This was more or less the nature of the exchange between us. At the beginning of her written work, Idit described what happened in her own words.

> Ever since I was a very little girl in first grade, I knew I would be a teacher when I grew up. I saw that my friends were indecisive about their futures. But for me, there was no sense of ambivalence" (Prologue, p. 8).

Idit wrote more than ten drafts of what she at first referred to as "the story of my life." The first draft began with the same story, which she saw as the "beginning." It was easy and convenient to begin by describing what had happened in first grade, as she more than once had declared that she had wanted to be a teacher since first grade. The first draft began like this:

> My first day at school. Excitement. Anticipation. First grade. A brand new year. Pupils gathered in the schoolyard. Children sitting on the ground. Ceremony to welcome the first graders.

> I clearly remember the two first grade teachers. I wanted the one with the pretty handbag whose hair was meticulously groomed in the bouffant style popular at the time. My happiness knew no bounds when I was assigned the teacher I wanted so badly. Today children usually meet their teacher a day before school starts to make it easier for them to adjust as they enter first grade. That wasn't the case then. Everything was new and very big for me. I remember first grade as a year of anger, anger, and more anger. When I think about it in retrospect, that teacher did not like children who talked out of turn. I liked to talk to my friends, and apparently was more than just chatty— I talked all the time. The teacher would come to class in the morning, stand in the doorway, and, before even saying good morning, she would send me to stand in the corner.

This draft went on to describe additional anecdotes from her elementary school years. Even in this early draft, Idit tended to view each incident from the perspective of "then" and "now." For example, when describing herself as a child who was not one of the first grade teacher's favorites, she also brought up an incident from her current class involving a boy who was not very popular among his schoolmates, to say the least.

This year I am teaching fifth grade. During the summer vacation, the principal phoned me, very agitated. The mother of one of the pupils who was supposed to be in my class had called her and announced she was transferring her son out of the school. Why? Because he felt rejected and unpopular. All the time there were accusations that he was violent, did not study, and other such complaints. The mother felt she could not cope any longer. She planned to transfer him to another school with the idea that if you change your place, you change your luck. I was superficially acquainted with this pupil from school. I asked the principal to set up a meeting between me and the mother. We met—the mother, the boy and me. He's a charming and good-looking kid. We spoke, and I asked the mother to give me a chance to restore her son's sense of security. She agreed. Today this boy is one of the most popular pupils in the class. He's a good student, and there's been a change, practically a complete turnaround, in his behavior.

In this first draft, Idit also described two critical events from her elementary school experiences. The first occurred in first grade and involves the first grade teacher, while the second took place in the fifth and sixth grades, with a teacher she defined as a "teacher for life." The draft also included a number of shorter descriptions of other events in her life, but for the most part focused on events from the present to help accomplish her goal of shedding light on her fundamental nature as a teacher today.

In my role as her thesis advisor, I wrote her the following note in response to the first draft.

Idit,

Your writing is moving and generally depicts a clear picture of your learning experiences in elementary school and the teachers' seminary. (Since you skipped over your experiences in high school, I assume they did not leave any impression on you.) Nevertheless, at this stage your writing is quite spontaneous and not organized, as is to be expected from a first draft. At this point, you should concentrate on two things.

First – Structure of the text. For example, you can construct your story in one of two ways:

A. Interweaving of stories from the past with stories from the present. That is, discuss how an event from the past influenced an event in the present, and examine how this is explained by the theoretical literature that you review in the chapter. I believe you favor this structure, and there is no problem in applying it to the text you've used here.

B. Telling the stories from the past in sequence, and after that, in a separate chapter called something like "To Be a Teacher," explaining what kind of teacher you are today in view of what you experienced in the past. You can begin this structure with a selection of the anecdotes you tell throughout the story, and then try to interpret your fundamental essence as a teacher from what you cite from the theoretical literature. Finally, you can "close" the circle with you own interpretations of what influences you today as an adult.

Choosing a structural framework for the story is up to you. As it stands now, your chronology is unclear, and you repeat things that could be grouped together. I marked the anecdotes describing stories from the past in gray, mainly for myself so I could follow what was happening.

Second – identifying the topics you want to investigate in the theoretical literature. I think it would be appropriate for you to read about the "good teacher." Even though you've already researched this topic, it would be a good idea to expand your investigation, including the teacher's role as "educator" and the pedagogy of liberation that you began to write about. Further, you should look into the subject of parent-teacher relations, which emerges strongly from your story.

You explain very well why you behave in one way today and not another, and you do not need any suggestions for these interpretations. You can, however, perhaps glean some further insights from the literature. Both the theoretical and the research literature can help you learn more about yourself as a teacher who is sensitive to the "other" simply for being human.

Please note my remarks in the left margin.

Sincerely,

Hanna

As her advisor, I called her attention to two matters. First, I pointed out the need to enrich her discussion of events from the past. Second, I recommended ways of presenting past events so they shed light on present occurrences. In addition, I directed her toward identifying major themes that she might like to read about further in the theoretical literature to help her interpret what happened in her professional life. Indeed, by its very nature autobiography is not merely the story of a life. If it were, it would remain in a purely narrative form, and would be no different from Ashton-Warner's story in *Teacher* or McCourt's story in *Teacher Man*. The "critical" part of critical autobiography, in contrast, involves surveying the theoretical literature as well as being able to take a step back and observe one's professional life rationally. My reason for presenting my interactions with the teacher-inquirer is to support my claim that the advisor plays a crucial role in building and writing a critical autobiography. The advisor helps the teacher-inquirer distance herself from these moving events that occurred in her life and promotes her ability to examine her life story systematically and logically.

The spontaneity in writing the first draft is typical of all who undertake to write critical autobiographies, and it is unavoidable. Without this spontaneity, the researcher cannot set off on the journey. A life story does not have a "beginning, middle and end," and the critical aspect of autobiographical writing is not prearranged and known in advanced, for if it were, there would be no need for research. Idit began her research journey with a first draft that gave direction to her research: to position incidents that happened when she was a child in school against events from her life today as a schoolteacher. Not every critical autobiography is written like this. This is an example of the choice the writer has in selecting the direction for developing her autobiography.

At some point, we made a decision to print the stories from Idit's past in italics, while the stories from the present would appear in regular font. The reason for this was to make it easier for the readers to distinguish between past and present events. The following section shows how two stories were presented one after the other—one from the past and the other from the present. Both included the teacher's interpretations based on observing these events from her present perspective:

Pasternak (2002) argues that the family makes an important contribution to a child's success in school. She believes that the determining factor is the emotional atmosphere in the home and the extent to which the parents provide their children with emotional, social and instrumental resources. I see myself as responsible for my pupils and for their educational achievements. Hence, I rarely recommend going to tutors. I do so only in cases where the system cannot provide a solution, for example severe learning disabilities that I cannot cope with, and even this I do with a heavy heart. I believe that all teachers should receive training in special education so they can have the tools to help children who are having difficulties.

Every day I experience difficult moments alongside moments of satisfaction. I love going into the classroom to teach, and I enjoy interacting with the children. I have a lot of trouble dealing with school politics, with parents who look for ways to interfere, and with dishonesty. It is the little successes that have kept me in the teaching profession. Every day I experience things that bring me pleasure.

I have always wanted to be a teacher. *When I was in first grade, I had a blackboard with chalk. I used to go into my room, sit my dolls down in a row, and begin yelling and cursing at them. My mother told me that that was how she knew what was happening at school. My nasty and harsh language unmistakably brought home what had been happening in class.* Today, when a teacher tells a child to shut up, the parents show up at school the next day complaining that their child has been insulted. *When I was in school, it was unheard of to complain or phone the teacher at home; all you could do was hope to get through the day safe and sound. In the fourth grade, I took ill and missed ten days of school. I recovered, and the doctor gave me the okay to return to school. A field trip to Jaffa was planned for the next day, a Tuesday. When we got home from the doctor on Monday, my mother called the school secretary and asked to speak to T, my teacher, explaining that I had been ill. I don't remember the teaching calling to ask how I was.* Today if a child misses more than three days of school, the teacher must phone to find out what is wrong. *My mother asked the teacher what she thought. Should she send me on the trip, as approved by the doctor, or should she keep me home one more day? The teacher said it would be a pity to miss the trip, and that of course she should send me to school. I was happy to go to school. We set out on the trip. I was at the end of the line, with the teacher and an accompanying parent behind me. Near the clock tower in Jaffa, I overheard the teacher saying to the parent, "She doesn't come to school, but they send her on field trips." How the rest of the trip was for me goes without saying. I came home feeling highly insulted. After all my mother had asked the teacher, and the teacher said I should come. How mean of her! How hypocritical! I guess I cried, because my mother opened the phone book, intending to call the school. She was extremely angry. I remember begging her not to call. I didn't want any further arguments. In the end my mother did not call. I guess she felt I'd suffered enough abuse and didn't want to add insult to injury.* I remember this incident, as if engraved on my heart. I never talk near the children, and I always ask the other teachers not to talk out loud and to watch what they are saying. Sometimes you can unintentionally cause permanent damage.

For six years I taught mixed classes in which children diagnosed with learning disabilities were mainstreamed with children without such disabilities. The class had two teachers, a special education teacher and a regular teacher—me. Teaching a mixed class is a real experience. I learned quite a bit during those years, from my co-teacher who became my good friend, and from the pupils. We taught one class for two years and the other for four years, from first to fourth grade. The pupils from the second class are now in the eleventh grade. When that class graduated from the ninth grade, the father of one of the boys who had been mainstreamed called me and proudly reported that his son had successfully completed the ninth grade. To a large extent, he attributed his son's success to me as his teacher. My faith in the child and my confidence that he would overcome the obstacles gave the parents and the pupil as well the strength to cope. Now this boy is successfully finishing the eleventh grade. I believe that the fact that my teachers did not encourage me brought me to where I am today, to my perspective on school and its role in children's lives which differs greatly from that of many of my teaching colleagues. Life is not easy and often confronts us with difficult trials, so that it's important to make things easier whenever possible. I try to make things easier for my pupils in whatever way I can.

In this draft, Idit identified the themes she wanted to examine and then set out to research them in the theoretical literature. She read about how people choose the teaching profession, what makes a "good" teacher and educator, and the type of pedagogy she identified as "her" pedagogy, i.e. Freire's pedagogy of liberation. She even read about parent-teacher relations, a topic clearly relevant to her life story in the past and the present as well. She disengaged herself from the events of her life, applying what she had discovered in the literature in order to explain and better understand events from her past and from the present. Gradually she began to integrate her research findings in interpreting the various events of her life. The text had become more profuse and longer, but was still unfocused.

During the ongoing process of writing, advisor response and revision, Idit added additional chapters, each focusing on a different topic. Eventually, she decided upon the following chapters, based upon the work's major themes:
– Choosing the teaching profession
– Teaching as leadership
– Teaching as a force for empowerment and caring in a multicultural society
– Teaching as a mission
– Parent-teacher relations

After Idit divided her work into these chapters, she found it easier to delve more profoundly into the theoretical literature according to the developing themes of her critical autobiography. Ultimately, the opening of Idit's autobiography was quite different from that of the first draft. She chose to begin by discussing the choice of the teaching profession. Following are the initial paragraphs of the first chapter of her thesis:

Choosing the Teaching Profession

The choice of a profession is among the major decisions individuals must make over the course of their lives. It is a decision that has diverse implications, among them psychological, social and economic. I chose to become a teacher based upon a number of considerations, the most important of which was that I had wanted to be a teacher since the first grade. I always knew I would become a teacher. Psychologists claim that the choice of a profession is what defines individuals and makes them unique. It is what will determine their social standing and often what will define how they relate to other human beings as well (Klegman, 1973).

I did my military service[20] at a military recruiting station, and I became close friends with two physicians serving there.[21] We would spend hours talking. When I mentioned I was planning to study to become a teacher, one of my friends belittled the idea of studying at a teachers' seminary. These seminaries were not prestigious enough. My friends tried to convince me to go to university.

Teachers appear to have a low public image. This may stem from the fact that many women become teachers because the work is "convenient" when they have young children. The work hours and vacations are very enticing. The teaching profession has traditionally been considered a woman's profession (Perry, 2004), and the role of women in teaching has always been complex. It is a feminine profession. Women are identified with child care (Oram, 1989). Traditional society believes women are suited for teaching in elementary school. They are maternal and thus naturally suited to care for children (Griffin, 1997). Indeed, the younger the children, the greater the percentage of women caring for them. The teaching profession is seen as the continuation of housework and childcare, thus bridging the gap between the private and public spheres. Hence, women teachers are expected to safeguard society's values, just as women at home preserve the existing social order and traditional values (Oram, 1989).

Idit's critical autobiography comes full circle at the end of the entire written study, where she discusses this same topic:

> Recently I spoke with my physician friend who had served with me at the recruiting station and had put down the seminary as not being prestigious enough. We spoke about my work, and he expressed his desire for me to teach his children. As I think back on our discussions then, I do not believe he still belittles the teaching profession. One of my closest friends is a famous and successful career woman who appears in front of large audiences every night. When I told her I was going for my master's degree, she said, "Finally I'll have a friend with a master's degree." I admire her so much for her achievements and her colorful career, and here she is, thinking I'm the one who has achieved great things in accordance with the old saying, "The grass is always greener on the other side of the fence." At this point in my life, I believe the grass on my side is greener!!!

This conclusion enabled Idit to choose the overall topic for her work: "In spite of and regardless of everything—a teacher." Only after coming full circle and reaching the insight that "the grass on my side is greener" was Idit able to understand that she is a teacher "in spite of and regardless of everything." This declaration and the use of the metaphor "the grass on my side is greener" are expressions of liberation. Indeed, Freire has already declared that writing is often an expression of liberation that enables the writer to shed light on the past from the perspective of the present. I am not referring here to just any form of writing, but rather to what an individual writes about his or her own life. In his book *Letters to Christina* Freire (1996) claims:

> For me to return to my distant childhood is a necessary act of curiosity. In doing so, in stepping back from it, I become more objective while looking for the reasons I involved myself and these

reasons' relationship to the social reality in which I participated. It is in this sense that the continuity between the child of yesterday and the man of today is clarified. The man of today reflects in order to understand how the child of yesterday lived and what his relationships were within the family structure, in the schools, and on the streets (p. 14).

The past, then, is analyzed through the eyes of an adult "knower"—that is, an adult with knowledge and understanding—from the perspective of the present day, thus revealing the continuity between the child of yesterday and the adult of today. The ability to observe past events through the eyes of an adult and to reach new insights, even if the memories are not always an exact copy of what actually happened in the past, is part of the liberation discussed by Freire.

Idit's writing process had ended but was not yet complete. She had divided her story into chapters, had given each chapter a name, and had used logic and perspective to link what had happened in the past to what she is today and to what was described in the theoretical literature she had examined. And yet, something still seemed to be missing. The work appeared to need a prologue describing what preceded the writing process, as well as an epilogue describing what is happening now that she has finished the thesis. Though this was not an easy task, it was essential. Idit needed to come full circle and see the entire picture of the story of her life and its implications on her teaching today. Following are the prologue and epilogue of Idit's thesis:

Prologue

From the time I was a very little girl in first grade, I knew I would be a teacher "when I grew up." I saw my friends vacillating about their futures. I had no such uncertainty. I decided to enroll in a teachers' seminary. After completing my studies there, I immediately began teaching. I've been a teacher for twenty years. I have always loved teaching. In my first years of teaching, I encountered teachers who were weary and burnt out, and I promised myself I would never get to that point. I knew that as soon as I felt myself burning out, I would look for other work. Today, twenty years later, I still feel I have much to contribute to the educational system. I feel neither burnt out nor fatigued. I decided to write the story of my life to examine and better understand myself. During my years of teaching elementary school, I often found myself frustrated. To my great amazement, those experiences of frustration did not embitter me. Rather, they caused me to want to make a difference, to change things in some modest way in my own little piece of heaven on earth. When I was in school, I had more than a few negative experiences, and in my work I try to mend and fix things, to somehow make things better Strain (1971) stated that the direction is determined by the child's developmental stage and by the quest for complete and multifaceted personal development. . . . I believe that children are like clay in the hands of the potter. We have the power to give them the space to grow so they can each find the most appropriate path in life. These results can be achieved only through understanding and compassion. I have decided to write the story of my life to help other teachers interested in this approach to understand and feel what their pupils are going through. Sometimes we teachers forget the extent to which we can influence the children. We are dealing with matters of crucial importance. Sometimes our daily routine takes over and we tend to forget this. The objective of my research is to help make us aware of what we know but often forget.

For me, writing this thesis has been a journey into the depths of my being. I have studied events from the past in an attempt to understand my professional development and the way I have conducted myself as a human being, as a mother and as a teacher.

Epilogue

Today, after having written my critical autobiography, I can indeed state that I have come full circle. I have resolved my anger and settled my accounts with those in the educational system. I have gained new insights and knowledge, and I have the desire and energy to do things differently, better, more appropriately and with more sensitivity. Leiblich (2005) claims that an individual writes the story of his life to liberate himself from his past. In some sense I can say that writing the story of my life has liberated me from my constant and enduring anger at teachers who taught me in the past. Freire (1996), too, maintains that writing is liberating, and that certainly is the case. I feel as if I have "sent away" my anger, banished it to some other place.

Writing my autobiography and being exposed to information sources clarified things for me and provided me with new insights about my choice of the teaching profession and my work as a teacher. While I was writing, I learned a great deal about myself. My faith was strengthened that I had indeed done the right thing. Richie and Wilson (2000) maintain that writing enables teachers to carry on a dialogue with what they have written, to carry on an internal debate and to improve. According to Richie and Wilson, the more teachers write, the more they are capable of redesigning and establishing anew their personal and professional experience. My feeling is that I have indeed gone through a process. The labor of writing cannot be completed overnight. It involves thinking about matters and internalizing them, understanding and accepting them. I learned there are things I have the power to change, and that I must do my utmost to change them. And there are other things that are beyond my power to change, so I must try to accept them. I believe that my future teaching will be different, based on new insights . . . .

The search for truth and justice was an integral part of the way of life in the home in which I grew up. For me teaching is a way to fulfill my potential. It is the natural outgrowth of my quest for truth and justice, for myself and for those around me.

Idit's critical autobiography is not cited here in its entirety, for what is of interest here is the story of the process of writing the autobiography under my guidance. In directing Idit, my goal was to show how the writing process is an inherent part of a teacher's self-study and can assist her in developing her sense of professional self.

"In My Work I Try to Fix Things, to Make Things Better" – A Narrative of Growth

Idit's critical autobiography is her personal and professional narrative. Her narrative is interspersed with stories from her childhood related to her experiences at school and how she was educated at home, as well as to instructional situations from her experience as an elementary school teacher. The past in her story sheds light on the present, and the prologue she ultimately used as the beginning of her story is in fact a summary of what she today considers the insights she gained from the story of her life. The opening sentence, "From the time I was a very little girl in first grade, I knew I would be a teacher 'when I grew up,'" was written not out of uncertainty or skepticism but rather out of a sense of understanding and fulfillment. In contrast, the statement she made to me before opting to write her autobiography and learn the reasons that led her to be a teacher and the person she is today was said out of a sense of puzzlement. At that time, it was not at all clear to her why "in spite of and regardless of everything" she had always wanted to be a teacher. Now, after having examined her own life, she makes this same statement out of a sense of understanding, which clearly emerges in the following two sentences. "I saw my friends vacillating about their futures. I had no such uncertainty." Her language is firm and decisive, as reflected in the verbs and adjectives she uses: "I decided to enroll in a teachers' seminary." "I immediately began teaching." She then makes the following assessment: "I have always loved teaching. . . . I still feel I have much to contribute to the educational system. I feel neither burnt out nor fatigued." She candidly interprets the relationship between her childhood experiences in school and the teacher she is today. "To my great amazement, those experiences of frustration did not embitter me. Rather, they caused me to want to make a difference, to change things in some modest way in my own little piece of heaven on earth. . . . in my work I try to mend things, to somehow make things better."[22] Idit's use of the word "mend" has mystical undertones. She immediately follows it with supporting evidence from the theoretical literature to convince the readers and herself as well that "the direction is determined by the child's developmental stage and from the quest for complete and multifaceted personal development."

Idit's sense of her professional self emerges from the figurative language she uses throughout the story, whether consciously or unconsciously as is typical of metaphorical language. She refers to her work as a teacher as her "own little piece of heaven on earth" and sees it as an attempt "to mend and fix" the childhood injustices she experienced in school. She sees writing her thesis as a "journey into the depths of my being." She explicitly states that her adult persona has been shaped by the "landscape" of her childhood. In her teaching today she builds her lessons together with the children, "layer upon layer," stating that more than once "we sailed to places I never believed we would reach." The education she believes in is "liberating." It has the ability to "pave the way to the world of girls and boys . . . and give rise to the vision of a new destiny." At one point, she makes the following statement about the dialogue between her past and her current professional life: "As time goes by and the pictures become clearer, I am able to analyze and understand my behavior as a teacher." The "pictures," as she now refers to the events from her past, "become clearer"—indicating a change for the better, and perhaps growth as well. She ends her critical autobiography with "the old saying, 'the grass is always greener on the other side of the fence.' At this point in my life, I believe the grass on my side is greener!!!" (The exclamation marks appear in the original.)

It is interesting to examine the origins of her figurative language. On the one hand, she uses metaphors related to traveling and building, while on the other hand her figurative language refers to the surroundings of home ("little piece of heaven" and "grass"). Perhaps her use of travel metaphors and metaphors of building reflects her feeling of ongoing development and progress in her professional life. The metaphors related to the home environment serve to bring the teaching profession to her doorstep, to her place of safety and refuge. The profession is part of her, close to her, within her most intimate surroundings—home.

The epilogue, written in retrospect after the critical autobiography was completed, opens with the following metaphor: "Today . . . I have come full circle." It ends with her vision: "For me teaching is a way to fulfill my potential. It is the natural outgrowth of my quest for truth and justice for myself and for those around me." The closing of a circle, the road to fulfill-ment, and the continued quest for truth and justice—all these are picturesque expressions emerging from the consciousness of the teacher-inquirer at a particular point in the present. They underline her understanding and insights and stress the fact that the end of her writing marks the beginning of her work with a new perspective on her profession, and even the possibility of realizing her vision. The written narrative is complete, but the writer's professional narrative, which has become personal as well, continues to develop. Indeed, this is a narrative of growth.

GALIT'S CRITICAL AUTOBIOGRAPHY: A JOURNEY INTO MYSELF—FROM MY KIBBUTZ CHILDHOOD UNTIL TODAY[23]

The second critical autobiography in this chapter differs from the first. It focuses on the childhood of a teacher-inquirer who was raised on a kibbutz[24] until the age of seven and on the impact of the events of her early childhood on the kibbutz not only on her work as a teacher but on her personality as well. In her story she attempts to come to terms with her parents' political ideology, which governed how they, and she, led their lives. Indeed, it is apparent that this political ideology is still exerting its influence on them today. This is the story of a teacher, now in her late thirties, who decided to examine what led her to be what she is today, not only professionally but also as an individual and as a member of her family. In effect, she had unfinished business with her parents, which she managed to put in order by the end of her self-study. In writing about her attempts over the years to talk to her parents about her childhood on the kibbutz, she states that the discussions "were like probing an open and painful wound." "On those rare opportunities I had the guts and the emotional strength to confront them [parents] about these matters [childhood experiences], the discussions would become highly emotionally charged and I would end up hurling accusations." By the end of her study, Galit discovered her parents had the "courage and willingness to explore the emotional experiences they had gone through over the years."

Galit has been a teacher for fifteen years and is a former school principal. Currently she works as an elementary school language education instructor. From the first moment she was given the opportunity to embark on a self-study, Galit knew she would examine the story of her life and its significance in shaping the person she is today: a teacher, a mother, a woman. As part of her studies for the M.Ed. degree in Language Education in a Multicultural Society, Galit enrolled in the graduate research seminar on Multiculturalism and Multilingualism. She was pleased to have the opportunity to use self-study to clarify what she called "the relationship between my personality today and my childhood on a kibbutz." In other words, she chose to examine "how my kibbutz childhood influenced the shaping of my adult persona today."

During the entire time Galit carried out her self-study, it was clear to me as her advisor that her research practically wrote itself, without any need for additional intervention by me. Unlike in the case of Idit's critical autobiography where I focused on the interaction between me as advisor and her as writer, here the writing flowed. Most of my guidance was in the form of providing feedback on the chapters, asking for clarifications, additions and clearer transitions between the narrative and theoretical sections. Therefore, Galit's critical autobiography is presented here from her point of view, with no description of our relationship as advisor and student.

Because Galit decided to concentrate on her early childhood, she could not rely exclusively on her memories, which were often hazy due to the time that had passed. Hence, her data collection included interviews with her parents, the significant adults in her life, as well as a diary written by the woman in charge of her group of children on the kibbutz documenting the development of each child in the group. This being the case, Galit's research tools in her self-study were not only memories, but also interviews and written documentation.

Galit's parents immigrated to Israel from France after they married and settled on a kibbutz, where Galit was born and lived until the age of seven. Galit's kibbutz childhood was characterized by the communal sleeping arrangements in the children's house, which evidently made a lasting impact on her. At the very beginning of her autobiography, she tells about what motivated her to examine her kibbutz childhood. The prologue of her work begins like this:

The following incident occurred three years ago. We were visiting my parents on a Friday night, together with friends from our time on kibbutz. During dinner, the kibbutz suddenly came up in conversation. I remember clearly that as soon as I heard the word "kibbutz" I burst out in anger and asked them, without any hesitation, "How could you agree to have your children live away from you, in a children's house?" All three of them tried to explain what was behind the notion of communal education and why they were drawn into it, but I was not prepared to listen or accept what they had to say. The discussion deteriorated into unpleasant tones, with me hurling out harsh accusations. I sensed their embarrassment but also their need to justify their actions.

She added an explanation of what motivated her to embark on this self-study at this particular point in her life and of the relation between the education she received and who she is today as an educator and a mother.

The older I got, the more I began to see I had grown up in a system of social values in which the kibbutz members sacrificed their own needs and desires for the good of the collective and its goals. While writing the story of my life, I understood I needed to delve into the willingness of the kibbutz members, including my parents, to sacrifice themselves, and often their children as well, for the sake of the kibbutz and the realization of their vision. As an educator, I was particularly fascinated by the communal sleeping arrangements, for it seemed to me that this was what demanded the greatest personal sacrifice for the common good. I was raised in this system up to the age of seven, and I grew up with the deep conviction that I would never be willing to raise my children under such an arrangement. To this day, I am still "burdened" by feelings of pain, anger and abandonment.

Galit's critical autobiography is divided into three main chapters:
- "The Journey Begins"—Immigration to Israel and Settling on the Kibbutz
- My Kibbutz Childhood
- "Stations along the Way"—The Passages in my Life

Galit chose to begin her autobiography with the biography of her parents, as she was convinced it would be impossible to understand her life without understanding what motivated her parents to immigrate to Israel and why they chose to live on a kibbutz rather than in a city. As she put together the chronological story of their immigration to Israel, she began asking questions about things she did not know. Which youth movement was it that her parents had belonged to when they decided to immigrate to Israel? What was this movement's ideology, and how did it affect young Jews? While investigating this period in her parents' life, she began researching relevant topics in the theoretical literature. These topics were integrated in the first chapter, in which she describes the immigration of her parents. She describes two idealistic, ideologically inclined young people aged 18-20 who believed they were doing what was just and right. Galit interspersed the chronological story with her own interpretations of her parents' life, as influenced by her survey of the relevant literature as well as her insights today as a married woman with children of her own. She interviewed both her parents, thus including them in her research. In fact, as her self-study progressed, it began to have an impact within her extended family, and her parents, brother, husband and children became partners to her research.

> My parents told me they made their decision to immigrate to Israel and join a kibbutz based upon the influence of the Hashomer Hatzair[25] youth movement on their worldview. They had been educated according to the movement's ideological foundations, which they believed in and identified with. Their longstanding membership in this movement instilled in them deep feelings of identity with the Jewish people, kibbutz values and the concept of communal living.

Because it was important for Galit to understand the concept of Jewish youth identifying with the ideology of a youth movement, she researched this topic, leading her to the following interpretation:

> Werner's (1996) study can to some degree shed light on the deep feelings of identification my parents and other young people felt for the values of the Hashomer Hatzair youth movement. The study examined what was so attractive about the youth movement that led its members to identify with it so strongly. Though the findings were not conclusive, for the most part one answer clearly stood out—the ideology. . . . At that time, personal identification with the movement was a peak experience that endowed young people with the self-image of someone with ideological awareness, a member of society's elite. . . . Even my parents admitted they believed they were of a higher standard than other young people who were not members of a youth movement.

From the outset of Galit's study, the communal education on the kibbutz was a sensitive issue. For this reason, Galit diligently researched this type of education in the theoretical literature. Fascinated by what she read, she did not make do with just this topic but went on to examine theoretical psychological models to try and explain her behavior as a child. "I was a stubborn kid and if I wanted something I would not give in. I wanted everything for myself. . . . I would get angry if [other children] did not want to play with me. At that point I began getting into fights with other children." In the following, she tries to explain her relationships with the other children in her cohort group based upon her literature survey:

> What I generally recall from that time is that I liked to be with other children my age, even though deep down I know it wasn't easy for me to be with them. There were many arguments, probably because of all the time we had to spend together. In this regard, Dar (1998) maintains that the centrality of the group [in kibbutz communal education] was a direct result of the reduced role of the family in the child's life and the relatively large amount of time the child spent in the children's house.

In practically the same breath, she projects this onto herself as an educator today:

> Even back then, I was already the image of a "little educator" with a highly developed sense of justice. I was always trying to settle other children's disputes and problems. I always had the desire to help. But I also remember moments of sadness, loneliness and longings for my parents, especially for my mother. From time to time, when I remember those moments, I can't help but feel some twinges of sorrow.

Consequently, she was interested in discovering how her parents felt about communal education. She interviewed them and discovered that at the time her mother believed -

> . . . that was the best way to raise children, and that the quality of time parents spent together with their children on the kibbutz was more important than the quantity of time city parents spent with their children while they were preoccupied with taking care of the house and making a living. She also felt it was advantageous that she as a woman, not just as a mother, had the opportunity to develop in directions that interested her, to contribute to the pioneering enterprise, and to spend more time with my father and their comrades . . . . Indeed, for my parents and their friends, the emphasis was on communal life, which they saw as an impetus for raising their children as socially involved individuals rather than as people who only took themselves into consideration. My father even saw this way of life as

part of the pioneering enterprise, for it freed them to engage in pioneering ventures.

Galit's story continues as she describes the factors influencing the ideology of the youth movement and the kibbutz. She concludes the chapter on kibbutz education as follows:

> In conclusion, I must admit that at first I felt shocked and angry. I had a sense of profound personal and family sacrifice, and a feeling of having been abandoned by my parents . . . . Yet after I spoke with my parents and after I "discovered" the theoretical literature and learned a great deal about the kibbutz and its ideology, I felt that I must find a way to forgive them. Today I respect them more than ever for adhering wholeheartedly to the ideal they believed in and for working to realize it. Nevertheless, I am not willing to accept the fact that they sacrificed time to be with their children for the sake of the pioneering enterprise.

The last chapter of Galit's autobiography, entitled "Stations along the Way," describes her life as an adult. She reviews her personal life from the time she left the kibbutz and grew up in the city until the time she got married and had children. The story of her professional life, including her studies and her various jobs in the educational system, is integrated into her personal life story. In this chapter she attempts to answer the following question: "How have the passages in my life affected who I am today?" As she examines these passages in retrospect, from her perspective as an adult and after having completed her self-study, she comes to the following conclusion. "Because at each station along the way I relinquished something 'old,' I built a 'new' persona for myself." Based upon the theoretical literature, she analyzes every period of her life after the age of seven, when she and her family left the kibbutz and went to live in the city. Through these explanations, she is able to clarify what happened, why she behaved as she did, and why her parents acted as they did. She believes that one of the reasons her parents left the kibbutz is connected to their taking a more sober look at the kibbutz ideology.

> The reason they left the kibbutz was that they looked more soberly at the concept of communal education. As Lieblich (1994) puts it, they began to disagree with the way their children were being raised, in particular with respect to the communal sleeping arrangements. As time went by, my parents began to feel the "sting" in those arrangements. Despite all the pioneering aspirations and pretensions, ultimately it was the women who were raising the children, while the

men worked in the productive jobs. My parents began to understand that the kibbutz system was no more than a copy of the bourgeois family structure . . .

The passage from kibbutz education to city education was not easy for the child Galit.

I remember very well that during my first year in the city I swore that when I grew up I'd go back to the kibbutz! I may have felt that way because of the trouble I was having adjusting to the city. I felt strange and lonely. I had to get used to a different style of life entirely, make new friends, and cope with new requirements at school. The city school made different demands of me than those I had been used to on the kibbutz.

In this vein, Galit recalls one passage in her life after another, explaining why each passage took place and interpreting why things happened as they did. Ultimately, the most important step in her educational career was her decision to leave her administrative post as a primary school principal after only a year on the job and to take a job as a language education instructor. She made this decision contrary to the recommendations of all the professionals surrounding her. A young woman like her, at the outset of her career as an educational administrator, does not usually make such a decision. She links her personal life to her professional choice as follows. "I discovered that what was really important to me, to Galit, was not a successful career with achievements and prizes, but rather a happy and intact life with my family. . . . The pace of life [as an instructor rather than a school principal] suits me. We are all more relaxed and happier, and most important of all – I've started to smile again . . ."

Galit dedicates one chapter of her autobiography to discussing what she discovered from her research. She analyzes her life and comes to the conclusion that all of the events in her life, not just those from her kibbutz childhood, contributed to shaping her adult identity today. She discovers something else as well – she is not the only woman who was traumatized by the communal education on the kibbutz. After reading studies on kibbutz communal education and books written by other former kibbutz members, she came to understand that "[other] adults have bad memories of the kibbutz communal sleeping arrangements: the insufficient responses of their parents to their emotional needs, the pressures exerted by those in their age group, and the constant demands of collective life in general." She also learned about her parents, the pioneering Zionist movement they belonged to, the concept of communal living, and the ideology governing the notion of communal education.

It may be that the pain of being separated from my parents as a child and the anger I had to cope with over the years as a result of this feeling of abandonment have actually strengthened me and made me the person I am today – a family woman first and foremost, and after that an educator and instructor. In fact, I am convinced that my personal identity has become clear to me through this narrative.

Galit explicitly states that because of her self-study, she has been able to come full circle. She understands now and can forgive, although some part of the pain of her distant childhood will apparently remain with her forever:

I have come full circle, starting from the deep inner pain I had felt for years and ending by virtue of examining my life story, enabling me to get to know my parents and the kibbutz ideology better and to understand how the environment in which I grew up affected my development and the shaping of my persona. Examining my life story even has brought me a sense of emotional serenity, which came over me when I finished writing. My study has helped release me from a sense of unease and from painful feelings . . . . Looking at my work "from the outside" I can certainly say that writing it has equipped me with new spectacles, through which the same scenes and memories from my past today, with the added perspective of time, look somehow different to me . . .

Galit explains her character today and her choice of the teaching profession in terms of her childhood experiences:

Perhaps growing up in a communal environment surrounded by my age-group peers enhanced certain characteristics within me, such as feelings of empathy for other people and the desire to help, educate, guide, be meaningful to others, contribute, influence and lead. Even the profession I chose—teaching, administration and now instruction— certainly has fulfilled those characteristics . . . . I know I am a strong person, and I act in accordance with my beliefs and my feelings . . . . The feelings of anger I had to cope with over the years have actually strengthened me and made me the person I am today – a family woman first and foremost, and after that an educator and instructor.

Indeed, Galit comes full circle with feelings of acceptance and understanding.

> My renewed encounter with my kibbutz childhood was like an
> exciting journey back to childhood—to the painful moments and the
> beautiful ones as well. Scenes, memories, and feelings I had repressed
> deep inside myself emerged out of the mists of my memories, through
> several filters. For years I had built walls inside myself to prevent
> them [the memories] from bursting out and hurting me.

Writing her critical autobiography led Galit to understand the step her
parents had taken when they chose to raise her on a kibbutz during the early
years of her childhood. It enabled her to come to terms with this decision
and to better understand who she is today – a family woman first and
foremost, and after that an educator and instructor. As she put it, she was
able to calm down a bit, but not entirely. Her self-study led her toward a
further search. Through her investigation, she was able to understand
rationally, not emotionally, that she was not alone in her struggle, and that
others in her age group had had similar experiences to those she had gone
through. Following her self-study and its concomitant insights, she decided
to continue exploring the topic of communal education on the kibbutz as
she had experienced it thirty years before and to compare it to kibbutz
education today. The epilogue of her critical autobiography, therefore, is in
essence a new research project combining quantitative and qualitative
methods. This research will become her master's degree thesis. In it she
will examine how her contemporaries who grew up on kibbutzim view
kibbutz education then and now.

I Built a 'New' Persona for Myself"—A Story of Acceptance and Self Renewal

The new Galit, the persona she describes in her critical autobiography, did
not emerge simply out of her self-study. This persona developed over the
course of her entire life, gaining momentum in recent years, particularly
with her decision to leave her administrative position, take the position as
an instructor, and go back to school for her master's degree. Still, her self-
study enabled her to distance herself from events she considered painful
and to come to accept the way she had been educated on the kibbutz. Galit
examined her life systematically, one step after another. She selected an
event from the past, wrote it up, researched it in the theoretical literature,
then went back to the event and interpreted it. Ultimately, she created a
puzzle made up of the critical events of her life and of her newfound
understanding of each of these events. Her new persona is ambivalent.
While she has accepted the past, the pain will always remain with her. She
states this explicitly as follows:

The memories that had previously faded with time changed colors and nuances . . . . Today I understand more and I am more forgiving. Yet the wounds will never heal. They will continue to play on my nerves. They will probably be with me for many years to come.

For Galit, the good and the bad live side by side. Her journey into her childhood was a journey to "the painful moments and the beautiful ones as well." The language she uses in her text reflects this ambivalence in her life. Pain and hardship are interspersed throughout the story, in different forms. She uses expressions of anger in evaluating the events of her life. "To this day, I am still 'burdened' by feelings of pain, anger and abandonment." Her discussions with her parents "were like probing an open and painful wound." During one particular conversation, she "burst out in anger." According to her, these discussions "would become highly emotionally charged" with "unpleasant tones." She talks about the need "to cope with the demons inside me, to break through the dam." Even when she reaches an understanding of what happened in her life, she still talks about the need to "pick up the pieces and start planning the rest of my life." Hence, semantic fields expressing anger, pain and fragility are interspersed throughout the narrative, often emerging from the metaphors and figurative language she chooses to invest in her naturalistic descriptions of the extent of her pain. This is evident in the sentences she chooses for the conclusion of her critical autobiography: "Yet the wounds will never heal. They will continue to play on my nerves."

The adjectives Galit uses to describe kibbutz communal education come from the semantic field of sacrifice and of the victim or injured party. In her view, the kibbutz represents a system of social values "in which the kibbutz members sacrificed their own needs and desires for the good of the collective and its goals." Not only did the kibbutz system sacrifice victims, but her parents did as well. Her attitude toward life on the kibbutz as a life of sacrifice comes up several times in her autobiography. The adults made sacrifices, and she, once a girl and today a woman, is the innocent victim.

On the other hand, Galit also uses words expressing relief and under-standing. Almost unconsciously she uses the metaphor "when one door closes and another door opens" to describe one of the passages in her life. In effect, this sentence reflects the ambivalence running through her story. She may come up against closed doors, but she is always relieved to find another door opening for her. Her choice of a title for her written essay reflects this notion more than anything else: "A Journey into Myself." This is a metaphor as well, though it differs from the others, for it is somewhat distanced from what she describes in her study, yet it touches upon her own self. Her statements about her research process also reflect this perception of understanding and acceptance. Already at the beginning, she notes that "I see this [carrying out a self-study in the form of critical autobiography] as a golden opportunity to examine the story of my life." It is a "golden opportunity" to set out on something good. Indeed, it is not only a golden opportunity, but also something that will make a contribution to her own life. "Writing my autobiography has given me a great deal . . . . writing has equipped me with new spectacles . . . ." Again she uses a metaphor, this time "new spectacles" to describe her acceptance and understanding in a way that seems strongest to her. It is not easy to select the exact words to describe emotionally charged situations. It is even harder to reveal them to others, among them your advisor and your colleagues in the research seminar, while writing your critical autobiography. Galit mentions this exposure and her considerations of "profit and loss." She is convinced that what she has gained from her self-study will triumph over what she has lost by revealing the secrets of her life to the others in the group.

At the end of her self-study, she arrives at what has the potential to resolve the ambivalence in her life: a sense of the power of her own self. "I came out stronger and strengthened," she writes. Hence, today she sees herself as a strong woman who has made the right decision out of her understanding that she is first and foremost a woman and a mother, and only after that an educator and instructor. She created for herself what she refers to as a "new persona" that emerged from the critical events in her life and the insights she developed, as well as from the process of writing her critical autobiography. As the advisor of her self-study, I can truly say that Galit was prepared to write her critical autobiography. This "golden" opportunity presented itself at the most appropriate time for her. She was already almost there, on the verge of needing and wanting to examine her life and its impact on her. The research seminar provided the trigger for her to embark on her self-study. Because she was ready to examine her life, her work practically wrote itself, with almost no outside guidance. As she progressed, she understood how to distance herself from what was painful and difficult and she knew how to evaluate what had taken place in a rational, thoughtful way. Throughout her journey into herself, she continued to grow and develop more and more.

ACTION RESEARCH

Action research is a form of research that meets the needs of educators who examine their educational work in action. It is marked by a number of recurring cycles of action. Each cycle involves planning, acting (implementing plans), observing (systematically), reflecting and then re-planning (Cohen, Manion, & Morrison, 2007). As such, action research is a powerful tool for change and improvement at the local level.

As a research method, action research has a particularly broad scope. It can be applied in almost every research design in which people must solve a problem. Action research can be conducted by a single teacher, by a group of teachers collaborating within a single school, or by teacher educators in conjunction with researchers who collaborate with others as well, for example school counselors, university departments and sponsors (Cohen, Manion, & Morrison, 2007).

Much has been written in recent years about action research. Indeed, the diversity of perspectives on the action research design is reflected by its many definitions. Cohen, Manion, and Morrison (2007) survey an impressive number of definitions, all of which emphasize independent, reflective and methodological investigation marked by a number of action research cycles. In this sense, action research is a dynamic and spiral process whose objective is to improve and change an existing situation, or in other words, an existing practice. The research begins by identifying an issue or problem to be considered, continues by determining the relevant topic and ends by proposing a plan to improve the situation (Carr & Kemmis, 1986). The research process also has a number of different approaches. Some focus on posing a question and arriving at a solution based on the research, while others regard research as an ongoing process built around cycles that, as mentioned above, are characterized by planning, action, observation, reflection, and then repeated cycles of this same process.

According to McNiff and Whitehead (2002), action researchers support the notion that inquirers can create their own identities and should enable others to do the same. Action research combines diagnosis, action and reflection, focusing on practical issues that have been identified by participants and which are somehow both problematic yet capable of being changed. To put this in more simple terms, the goal of action research is to encourage self-study among those in the field by means of developing critical reflection, learning from experience, and an ongoing process of formative evaluation, all in order to generate changes in practice (Hacohen & Zimran, 1999).

Basically, the goal of action research is to bridge the gap between research and practice (Cohen, Manion & Morrison, 2007). Kemmis and McTaggart (as cited in Cohen, Manion, & Morrison, 2007) point to the distinctions between action research and what teachers normally think about in their everyday teaching routine.

– Action research does not involve solving simple problems, but rather stating a problem and asking a question in order to better understand the professional world by means of change and by means of studying how to improve it.

– Action research is not the way teachers ordinarily think while they teach. Rather, it is more systematic and involves collecting evidence upon which reflection can be based.

– Action research is not research about other people. It is a form of research that people apply to their own teaching practice to help them improve what they do, including how they work for or with others.

Many theoreticians consider action research to be a form of critical implementation, or in other words, critical praxis. Praxis is defined by Cohen, Manion, and Morrison (2007) as "action informed through reflection, and with emancipation as its goal" (p. 302). The essence of this approach involves reflective observation during the course of action, based on understanding and interpreting social situations with the goal of improving them. In this regard, action research is considered emancipatory, for it empowers individuals and the social groups in which they participate, causing them to take control of their lives within the context in which they can advance their own interests (Kincheloe, 2003).

One of the difficulties typical of action research involves how to measure its degree of success. Successful action research is marked by a change in the action methods of those involved, for example teachers and principals, and often those in the broader school community. For teachers, the change can be in their desire to vary their teaching methods and to adapt them to the learning situations. Additionally, they may adopt a different perspective, that of educators-as-learners who renew and transform themselves and become conscious of the extent of their responsibility. Moreover, interpersonal communication between teachers and pupils can grow stronger, teachers can find a common language, and together they can build ways to promote educational systems and fit them to the communities they serve (Karnieli, 2003).

According to researchers such as Keiny (2006), or Kincheloe & Tobin (2006), action research can be thought of as a specific case of qualitative research, located at the end of the spectrum of involvement, for in action research the researcher has maximum involvement. Keiny, for example, believes that action research is part of a new world view known as the ecological world view, which has come to replace the positivist world view. According to this perspective,

> . . . the researcher is part of the context under investigation. The researcher interacts with other components of the educational system, among them knowledge, teachers, pupils and principals. The researcher, as such, is capable of observing from the outside, conceptualizing these interactions, constructing theoretical knowledge and being responsible for these newly built knowledge constructs (Keiny, 2006, p. 26).

Nevertheless, action research can also take the form of quantitative research, depending on the context and the problem and research question identified by the teacher-inquirer.

There are those who consider teamwork an important element of action research (for example, Keiny, 2006; Zellermayer & Tabak, 2004). The creation of a collaborative research group transforms the research partners into a "community of learners." In this community, participants learn through questions arising from their practice as the research evolves. This learning later helps teachers encourage their own pupils to learn and to develop into autonomous learners in their classrooms. Keiny (2006) points to three strategies of action research: putting work into action and implementing it in practice, observing by means of ongoing data collection, and reflection. Through these strategies, teacher-inquirers become more conscious of their own work habits and more willing to carry out the changes required for collaborating with "outside" influences. In Keiny's view, research in a group setting is highly effective and also increases teachers' willingness to generate change on their own.

Action research is a form of self-study, whether it is quantitative, qualitative or a mixture of the two. At its core is the researcher, either an independent investigator or a member of a research group, who examines the teaching environment with the purpose of improving it. Such a systematic examination of the act of teaching can ultimately empower teacher-inquirers to generate changes in their work environment. Action research requires the research skills of systematic self-observation, reflection and rational interpretation that bridge between practice and theory. Hence, it can be ascribed to the group of studies defined as self-study research, studies focusing on teacher-inquirers and their professional development achieved through academic inquiry.

Action research, implemented by the independent teacher-inquirer, is, in fact, built upon the basic instructional case analysis approach, described in Chapter 3. Indeed, it constitutes an additional and more advanced level, whose goal is to develop teachers' systematic ability to observe their teaching environment in real time. Ultimately, teacher-inquirers launch an action research in order to better understand their professional environment and to make changes based upon their new understandings and insights.

In this chapter, I discuss how action research plays a role in the professional and academic development of a teacher who serves as a district language arts instructor.

MALI - AN INSTRUCTOR-INQUIRER: "LANGUAGE ARTS EDUCATION – EDUCATION FOR LIFE"

The action research story described in this chapter is the story of a teacher-instructor who independently studied and examined a particular aspect of her current professional environment. The research grew out of the work of a teacher named Mali[26], who had been trained as a special education teacher and for years worked with special needs pupils integrated into regular classes. While she was carrying out her research, she served as the district language arts instructor in the special education supervision system. I therefore, refer to her in this chapter as the "instructor-inquirer." The research described here is part of the instructor-inquirer's involvement in developing and running a unique special education project with the goal of achieving integrative education in school. The project combined two educational programs: (1) language arts, whose goal was to nurture the four language modalities of talking, listening, reading, and writing as well as grammatical elements relevant to the learner's language; and (2) the Lev 21 program, a "preparation for life" program comprising four units for helping pupils with special needs prepare for life: social education, education for the work place, education for living in the community, and continuing education. The instructor-inquirer saw both of these programs as pivotal programs in the core curriculum formulated by the Special Education Department of the Ministry of Education. The need to integrate these two programs arose from what was happening in the field. Moreover, those supervising the special education schools recognized that integration was needed to make teaching more effective for pupils with special needs. They were also interested in making learning easier for these pupils, and in ensuring the relevance and authenticity of the school's teaching-learning curriculum.

A steering committee was set up to develop and run the program. This committee, comprised of the special education supervisor, national and district instructors in special education, the principal of the school where the experiment was taking place, and the teaching staff, proposed using action research to examine the program as it evolved and to facilitate its development. Mali, who that year was studying for her M.Ed. degree, decided to carry out the research together with the instructor for the Lev 21 program, who was to be her colleague in implementing the program. The objective of the research was to examine, in real time, the nature of the developing dialogue between the two instructors and to determine how this dialogue could contribute to advancing integrative education at the school. The research documented by the instructor-inquirer comprised two cycles, with the second cycle emerging from analyzing the findings and conclusions of the first. The study described in the following section is a short-term study whose aim was to examine a localized educational situation with the goal of improving the instructors' work and promoting a new project in the schools.

First Action Research Cycle

The first cycle: focused on formulating a collaborative instructional plan. The two instructors, Mali, the language arts instructor, and Dana[27], the Lev 21 instructor, met to discuss this matter. They recorded their meetings electronically, and Mali, the instructor-inquirer, also documented what was discussed and achieved at the meetings in her reflective journal. In effect, the research tools were these taped observations and the instructor-inquirer's reflective journal. Such tools are typical of qualitative research. The problem identified at the beginning of the study was how the two instructors should construct a dialogue in order to promote the project in schools. Therefore, the research question posed in the first cycle was as follows: *What are the distinguishing features of the dialogue developing between the instructors?* The instructor-inquirer put it this way: "I chose to study the dialogue developing between us by examining the features of our first discussion, in which we attempted to determine how to integrate teaching the two programs."

After the first discussion between the instructors, Mali was puzzled. She told me that she felt something had not gone right in the discourse with the other instructor, but she could not put her finger on what was wrong or why they had not made any progress in planning the integration of the two programs. In retrospect, she admitted the following:

During the first stages of the research, I felt things were ambiguous and uncertain. I felt I was not dealing with the essence of the project—the

115

integration of the two programs. [Today I understand] that this issue can be examined in the next cycle.

The ambiguity in the interaction between the two was the central issue at the outset of their joint planning. It seems that for Mali and her colleague it was important to systematically examine what had happened in their discourse and why the planning did not progress as they had expected. It was only after in-depth reading and systematic analysis of the data that the picture began to become clear. The data collected during the course of the first cycle called for two types of text analysis: qualitative content analysis as is customary in qualitative research for identifying the major themes in the discourse of the two instructors, and discourse analysis to examine how the discourse between them was conducted. Indeed, the content analysis examined "what" the two talked about, while the discourse analysis investigated "how" they spoke to one another.

Content analysis. The data pointed to three major themes characterizing the topics raised in the discourse. The instructor-inquirer wrote about these themes as follows:

The purpose of the first discussion between us, the two instructors, was to determine how we should act in guiding the integrative teaching of the two programs. The following themes emerged from this discussion: 1. what the teachers already know about the two programs and how they can be instructed to acquire more knowledge; 2. how the cooperative instructional model should be formulated; 3. how the two programs can be integrated, according to each participant.

She concluded the analysis section as follows:

The discussion about the integration between the two programs considered the research question instead of how the teachers should be instructed, with no specific expectation of arriving at clear and unequivocal answers. The discussion about what the teachers know about the two programs ended with a decision acceptable to both of us [that the teachers should gain more knowledge about the two programs and the way to integrate them]. In contrast, the discussion of the cooperative instructional model reflected a gap in our perceptions of instruction, which remained open during the first stage of the research.

Discourse analysis. The discourse in fact took the form of a formal conversation between two instructors whose purpose was to arrive at some sort of common understanding and agreement. Mali, the instructor-inquirer, felt it was imperative in her study to relate to how the dialogue was conducted. Hence, analyzing the discourse between the two is of particular significance as it affects the planning and choice of action in the second cycle. The discourse analysis included three especially prominent features of how the dialogue was conducted: 1. the frequent use of negative words; 2. the frequent use of first person singular pronouns; 3. the use of verbs expressing a particular stance. The instructor-inquirer comments on the findings of the discourse analysis as follows:

> We used the negative words "no" and "not" frequently to reject one another's opinions or to express our position on this rejection. Here are a few examples:
>
> Dana: *I do not think* it would be the right direction to say to them TIME OUT, let's learn the principles of Lev 21, let's review the main points of language arts education . . . *I do not want to waste* any time because the staff also will not take this in the right way.
>
> Mali: *I do not think* this will be considered a waste of time. We need to do both.

These negative words "no" and "not" are also used to express a position. Most of the positions taken by each one of them refer to the optimal instructional model that each instructor believes to be correct with respect to her area of responsibility and to the integration of the two programs:

> Mali: It's not right to see this as teaching a separate subject in class. It's not as if a subject-area teacher is going into the classroom to teach. It doesn't work like that. This is not like teaching a chapter in the Bible.
>
> Dana: If you are already discussing this with the homeroom teacher, we can begin to talk about how we see the integration because I do have an idea of what to do. I don't want to impose this on the homeroom teacher. I want us to facilitate this one step at a time. I don't want to tell them, okay this is the Lev 21 Program and this is the language arts program, how do you think the two should be integrated? I want to provide them with a few other solutions, after we have brainstormed this together and discussed how we believe the two programs can be combined. I think it is extremely valuable for us not just to arrive and lay down what it is they should do. Let's observe them first.

After analyzing the discourse, the instructor-inquirer summarized the two analysis methods (content analysis and discourse analysis) as follows:

In concluding the first action research cycle, it can be said that the discourse analysis was in keeping with the content analysis. The major themes emerging from the content analysis reflected differences of opinion and a lack of agreement between us. This lack of agreement also clearly emerged from the discourse analysis, which was marked by expressions of negative positions. In my reflective journal as well, I expressed my feeling that I needed to stick to my opinion, to protect the territory of my knowledge and my "sense of professional self" as an instructor.

The instructor-inquirer interprets the first cycle as a fight between two deer, suggesting the metaphor of *deer locking their horns*. The dialogue is characterized as a dialogue in disguise or a pseudo-dialogue, in which each participant is entrenched in her own position. Their exchanges of words during the dialogue sound like this:

In my view, we . . .

Language arts education is another story . . .

I don't think we should be concerned with knowledge only . . .

I don't see that if . . .

It does not work like that!

The instructor-inquirer makes the following clarification.

The dialogue presented here is 'dialogue as conversation' as defined by Burbules (1993), in which each of us presents her point of view . . . , becomes entrenched in her positions, guards the territory of her area of knowledge, and does not relate at all to what the other is saying.

After the first action research cycle had been put into effect, the two instructors were able to identify the problem between them. It was then that Mali could share her new understandings and insights with her colleague, Dana. It became clear to both of them that the second action research cycle needed to provide a solution that would emerge from both instructors, and particularly from how the dialogue between them was conducted. Hence, they decided upon an action strategy to be applied in the second cycle.

Second Action Research Cycle

The second cycle: emerged from the first action research cycle. Based on the first cycle's findings, the two instructors decided upon their next action. They defined the way in which the lessons at the school would be integrated. The instructor-inquirer describes this new action as follows.

> Dana and I decided upon a plan of action. Every homeroom teacher at the school who was involved had to plan a lesson integrating Lev 21 and language arts. The lesson would be first planned with the help of the instructors, and would then be taught in the homeroom teacher's class, while the rest of the homeroom teachers would observe.

A new research question was then formulated: *How does the ongoing dialogue between the instructors reflect their method of instruction at school?* In formulating the question, the instructor-inquirer understood that "our primary objective in this research project is to achieve integrated teaching of the two programs by means of joint instruction by two instructors from different domains of knowledge." The new research question was examined through peer-to-peer collaborative learning by means of a feedback discussion between the two instructors and the teacher who demonstrated the integrated learning plan, with the other homeroom teachers also taking part. This feedback discussion was followed by a new dialogue between the two instructors, who discussed and analyzed the feedback discussion, this time between themselves. The meetings were taped and typed up.

As in the first cycle, this discussion was also analyzed using two methods: content analysis focusing on "what" the two instructors said during the feedback discussion and the subsequent dialogue meeting, and discourse analysis focusing on "how" the instructors spoke to one another with respect to the sample lesson and the feedback discussion. Since Mali was interested in the relationships developing between her and her colleague instructor, the analysis focused on the dialogue between the two instructors, as in the first cycle.

Content analysis. The content analysis revealed two major themes emerging from what the instructors said with respect to integrative teaching: 1. the main points of Lev 21 and language arts education in the lesson; and 2. the interaction among the pupils.

Dana referred to points such as "an initial event" which served as a trigger for further implementations in the classroom, and "an open conversation" related to that trigger. She also discussed the authenticity and relevance of the materials to the pupils' lives. Mali pointed to the language education elements emerging from the lesson, such as listening, talking, writing, reading and grammatical issues, and the way all those elements were used by the teacher and the pupils during the lesson. She claimed that writing was a missing element in the lesson and that the teacher should think about how to encourage the pupils to use writing in relation to the event they discussed. Each instructor clearly expressed her interest in the elements of "her" program, yet they both talked about integrating the two programs in one lesson.

Both instructors also mentioned how the pupils interacted and discussed each pupil's position within the community of discourse. Mali claimed that the two programs share this notion of how the pupil fits into the community of discourse, as both assume that a learner constructs knowledge within a supportive and active community of learners.

Discourse analysis. As noted, the discourse analysis focused on how the two instructors conversed with one another after the feedback discussion with the teacher who had given the lesson. The instructor-inquirer describes this dialogue as "generally using short sentences in which we seemed to complement each other by means of a) mutual agreement, expressed through cooperation in constructing the discussion, and b) questions that 'invite' the other conversant to take part in the dialogue."

The instructor-inquirer provides some examples of "cooperative and complementary sentences":

Mali: I am giving a seminar at the Local Resource Center for Special Education Services (MATIA).

Dana: So am I. Eventually we will be able to give a joint seminar on Lev 21 and language arts education.

Mali: We can show films and construct a joint format.

Dana: We can create a joint model.

Mali: So long as it's not fixed.

Dana: It will raise awareness [of integrating the programs].

The instructor-inquirer characterized the questions that arose in the dialogue by the two instructors as "questions of invitation." Following are some examples:

Mali: Should we set up joint meetings?

Dana: Yes, I think we should not necessarily make the meetings mandatory. Whoever wants to come, will come, and whoever doesn't, won't.

Mali: OK. Do you want to tell them when we will be here, and that whoever wants to is welcome to participate?

Dana: Yes . . . . When do you need to be at MATIA that day?

Mali: At 12:00

Dana: OK, then let's make appointments with some other teachers.

Mali: OK, it's settled then.

The instructor-inquirer summarizes the dialogue as "a dialogue that develops gradually, with each participant listening and paying attention to the other and completing her thoughts." She goes on to summarize the second cycle of action as follows:

> With the completion of the second cycle, we can say that there have been positive developments in the dialogue between us as instructors . . . the central themes emerging from the content analysis represent the interfaces between the two programs as they are reflected in the lesson, as well as the points we decided to emphasize in the feedback discussion. The discourse analysis also presents interfaces as expressed in the sentences of invitation and cooperation. The reciprocal ties between the content analysis and the discourse analysis are once again evident.

The instructor-inquirer describes the second action research cycle using the biblical sentence, "*And the wolf shall dwell with the lamb*" (Isaiah 11:1-10). The synergetic dialogue between the two instructors has become an interactive discourse. The instructor-inquirer characterizes the dialogue this time as a dialogue comprised of sentences of completion and invitation, as previously described.

The instructor-inquirer refers to this as a critical and liberating dialogue (Shor & Freire, 1987), a democratic form of communication that renounces control and reveals reality. In the following quotation from her work, the instructor-inquirer proposes her interpretation of the process occurring between her and the other instructor and discusses how their dialogue contributes to developing the integrative teaching program at the school:

> The research portrayed here testifies to the importance of professional relations among instructors who are in a cooperative instructional situation with the goal of having an impact on integrative teaching.

> Hence, it is essential to make the instructors aware of the importance of professional dialogue with a common goal . . . . Indeed, stressing the importance of the human element in the relations between those leading the programs can shed light on how to integrate the Lev 21 program and the language arts program into other educational settings as well as on inter-program integration in general . . .

The result of the two action research cycles was the creation of a six-stage model for the instructors to work together. Implementing this model constitutes the third cycle to be developed by the two instructors during the course of their instruction. According to the instructor-inquirer,

> documenting the processes we implemented over the course of the year enabled us to write up an instructional model for integrating the two programs. We demonstrated this model for instructors from other districts as well as for instructors on the national level . . .

DEVELOPING A SENSE OF PROFESSIONAL SELF THROUGH ACTION RESEARCH

The obvious question for the reader to ask now is the following: Why did Mali feel she needed action research? Why could she not have simply continued with her job of instructing teachers how to integrate language arts teaching when working on the Lev 21 program in their classes? My obvious answer is that Mali felt she needed the action research in order to clarify some highly embarrassing and ambiguous issues. One involved her relations with her colleague and how to sort out the dynamics of their joint instruction, in particular who is "in control" and how to be more flexible. The second was how to implement the "integration" of the two programs in school. Even though she was the instructor and was supposed to know the answer, she did not have an answer to this question. Through systematic examination of the discourse between the two instructors, Mali began to understand what was bothering her: the problematic relations between the two and the gap between their implementation perceptions. Examining their discourse carefully enabled them both to decide upon their next action: preparing a lesson with the teacher, and implementing this lesson as a study lesson for other homeroom teachers to observe and discuss. Looking carefully at the data from the second cycle enabled the two instructors to arrive at new understandings, to generate new knowledge and to develop a six-stage model of joint instruction and integration. They may have reached this point anyway, perhaps with the help of external factors such as the district supervisor, but this might have taken longer, and it might have been carried out against the professional judgment and knowledge of each of them. Based on evidence collected in real time, in-action, they were able to gain new insights about their own beliefs and the possibilities for collaboration in order to achieve improved instruction in school for the sake of promoting the integrated program. They have not yet reached their ultimate goal, but they have definitely broken down the barriers between them and have come to realize how they can move forward in their professional enterprise. I can metaphorically conceive of their generated new knowledge as knowledge that dwells in the intermediate space lying between them and at the same time encompasses them as well.

Let us examine Mali's professional growth during her action research. As her specific action research is a form of qualitative research, the writing is primarily reportive in nature and accompanied by the inquirer's interpretations. The development of the instructor-inquirer's sense of professional self can be identified from this type of writing through three of the analytical devices employed in previous chapters: positioning, evaluation and language.

In general, two directions of professional growth can be identified in this research:
– From ambiguity to scholarly academic clarity.
– From pseudo-dialogue to synergetic and communicative dialogue.

From Ambiguity to Scholarly Academic Clarity

At the outset, the position of the instructor-inquirer with respect to the research is notable both for her sense of insecurity and for the considerable ambiguity she feels. The research is not what she had originally thought it would be. "I felt things were very ambiguous and uncertain . . . ." Action research by its very nature generates dependency on others in the workspace of the teacher/instructor who is also the inquirer, for educators do not work independently or in a vacuum. In this regard, the inquirer states the following:

> During the course of the research, I was dependent upon the steps we took and on processing and analyzing the data, all of which led to the next action research cycle. This process involved a great deal of uncertainty at different points, as well as dependency on others to do what needed to be done. The work in the educational field was dependent on the human element and limited by the time we had at our disposal.

By the end of the study, the research process became clarified and academic confidence was regained. "[I understood that the integration of the two programs] could be examined [in the future] in the third action research cycle." During the course of the research, the instructor-inquirer used clear expressions of evaluation representing the professional confidence she had gained from the academic perspective. "As time went by, the methodology became clearer to me, and I felt more comfortable to let myself be directed by the findings and the data analysis." Furthermore, after she completed two action research cycles, she finds herself able to make use of her personal experience as a teacher-inquirer in her work as instructor by aspiring to encourage the teachers she instructs to become teacher-inquirers themselves.

> I feel that my experience in action research has fortified me in my role as an instructor-inquirer and has improved my professionalism. I use the action research methodology to help those I instruct to think like teacher-inquirers who document their work and transform it into public knowledge. As a result of my research and my examination of the theoretical literature, *I believe it is extremely important to teach educators to think like researchers.*

Hence, in the third cycle of this action research, the instructor-inquirer will likely focus on how she guided the teachers throughout the course of the action research. It will be based upon her newly found insight that educators should "think like researchers." In that sense, Mali expands the cycle of action and draws in other inquirers who will take part in the educational enterprise. Eventually, several cycles of action will develop concurrently, and a collaborative action research will emerge. This kind of collaborative action research gains its momentum in the educational arena. It is described, for example, by educational researchers such as Zellermayer and Tabak (2004), who point to three cycles of study in a partnership between a school and a teacher education college: that of the teachers, that of the student-teachers and that of the pedagogical instructor.

In Mali's case, her action research is the first trigger, which in turn can spread and impact other educators and draw them into their own cycle of action research. In effect, the process described by Cohen, Manion, and Morrison (2007) actually emerges: "Action research starts with small groups of collaborators at the start, but widens the community of participating action researchers so that it gradually includes more and more of those involved and affected by the practices in question" (p. 300).

Mali now perceives her role as an instructor not just as someone who "tells" teachers what to do, but also as someone who guides them in examining their own work and supports them in constructing a community of inquirers.

From Pseudo-Dialogue to Synergetic and Communicative Dialogue

The dialogue between the two instructors changed from a pseudo-dialogue, in which the two speakers primarily spar with one another, to a synergetic and communicative dialogue, in which the two speakers mutually complement one another and invite each other to continue speaking.

At first, the dialogue between the two is, in the instructor-inquirer's words, "a dialogue of the deaf" that resembles two deer locking horns. To her this metaphor represents what is going on between the two of them. It reflects how she positions herself in the instructional format—as someone who has firm opinions of her own and will not allow others to invade her well defined territory. This sort of positioning can be referred to as professional egocentrism. Her ability to use a metaphor heightens her awareness of what had previously been ambiguous and had left her feeling uncomfortable after the first discussion between the two. "Each becomes entrenched in her positions, guards the territory of her area of knowledge, and does not relate at all to what the other is saying." Analyzing the findings of the first cycle enabled the instructor-inquirer to become more aware of what had not been obvious at the beginning. The language she uses reflects this newfound awareness. At the end of the study, the dialogue has become, in her words, "a dialogue reflecting consent and collaboration." Moreover, she has become able to distance herself from the events and to analyze them using rational tools from her review of the theoretical literature. She regards the dialogue as a "critical and liberating dialogue," calling it "a democratic form of communication that renounces control and reveals reality." Perhaps more than anything else, the following evaluation expresses and sums up the growth in her perception of herself as an instructor:

> The concept of dialogue finds expression in my work both in the dialogue between the two programs and in the interpersonal dialogues that took place between Dana and me. After reading the transcripts of the meetings, I began to rethink how I express myself aloud, both with respect to the content of what I say and with respect to the nature of the discourse, word choice, linguistic register and how all these factors impact upon the person I am talking to.

The initial positioning of both instructors was, then, one of professional egocentrism, with each instructor entrenched in her own perspective and each viewing her area of expertise as the most essential element, neither one being able to consider the knowledge and needs of her interlocutor. As time went by, this positioning evolved into one of collaboration, so that a common ground was open and available to both fields of knowledge. This new positioning is apparently what enabled the instructor-inquirer to make the following unequivocal declaration at the end of the research: *"Dialogue between the instructors is an essential condition for joint instruction."*

CONCLUSION

This is how the instructor-inquirer characterized her own professional growth as a result of the self-study:

> I believe that the action research expedited the processes involved, for it sharply and clearly revealed behaviors that we would not necessarily have immediately paid attention to and led us to expedite change. I am convinced that such rapid change would not have occurred without the action research. The research forced us to read the transcripts of the discussions and the data analysis, often causing us discomfort. Moreover, in addition to this change, the differences of opinion between Dana and me at the beginning shook up my own perceptions about my own instructional procedures and caused me to reexamine my professional perspectives and my positions regarding my role as an instructor.

The instructor-inquirer set off on her research journey as a novice inquirer and a self-opinionated instructor with her own firm perceptions on the nature of instruction and the way it should be conducted. By the end—though not necessarily the conclusion—of the action research, she had used academic tools to generate new knowledge and insights about herself as an educator, the role of self-study in a teacher's growth and development, and the nature of instruction and how it should be carried out.

Action research, by its very nature, does not come to an end. In the third action research cycle, which is about to begin, the instructor-inquirer will be able to examine the question she had initially posed as she began her research: How can two programs be integrated and taught in classes for pupils with special needs, and what is the significance of this integration for the pupils? Moreover, by means of collaborative action research, the instructor-inquirer and her colleague instructor are both able to seek answers to this question, as are other teachers as well.

EPILOGUE: REVISITING SELF-STUDY
AS A NARRATIVE OF GROWTH

This book has described three approaches to self-study: analysis of instructional situations or cases, critical autobiography and action research. The aim of these three approaches is to facilitate professional growth among teachers by systematically researching the practice of teaching. As noted at the beginning of the book, self-study is perceived as a form of research in which teachers examine their beliefs and actions within the context of their work as educators. The aim of this form of research is to pose pedagogical questions for consideration, as previously pointed out by researchers such as Whitehead (1993), and to arrive at alternative solutions to problems arising in various teaching situations. Indeed, the prevailing belief over the past decade is that schools will develop concurrently with their teachers and should therefore encourage research and cooperation among teachers (McLaughlin et. al., 2008).

In addition to describing the ways in which teacher-inquirers pursue their research and the insights reached as a result of the academic process, the book proposes critical discourse analysis as an approach for revealing a teacher-inquirer's sense of professional self. Not only does the process of uncovering this sense of self assist teacher-inquirers in recognizing their professional identity as teachers at the outset of the research, it also facilitates the development of this identity over the research period or as a result of the study process.

Indeed, in this book self-study has been presented as a narrative of growth. First, self-study requires basic research skills and therefore constitutes an important first step into the world of research for the novice inquirer who aspires to conduct more complex research. Moreover, self-study is a powerful tool in facilitating professional growth among teachers. Finally, self-study utilizes a set of approaches and methodologies, among them instructional situations or cases, critical autobiography and action research.

In particular, the book has attempted to shed light on the following perspectives with respect to the issue of self-study:

- It has presented a variety of approaches to self-study, among them analysis of instructional situations ("cases of teaching"), critical autobiography and action research.
- It has described methodologies that teachers and researchers can apply to their teaching and research arenas.
- It has offered a new approach for utilizing and analyzing instructional situations through an examination of both "the authentic case of teaching" and "the expected case of teaching."
- It has provided a fresh view of critical autobiography as a powerful tool teachers can use to examine their own practice and professional development.
- It has introduced critical discourse analysis as a useful tool for researchers and educators, one that enables teacher-inquirers to discover their "sense of professional self" and their professional identity emerging from their practice.
- It has introduced the role of the teacher-educator as a relevant figure in the professional lives of teachers, indeed as a moving force motivating teachers and student teachers to engage in self-study.

Based upon the above perspectives, the following new questions can now be asked: How do the three approaches to self-study impact the field of teacher education? Furthermore, how does self-study affect the policies of decision-makers in the field of teacher education?

In my view, teacher education should move from practice to theory and back again, rather than the other way around. That is, in seeking to gain additional knowledge and insight about the practice of teaching, teachers and student teachers can look first at their own cases of teaching and their own personal biographies. Teachers or student teachers can first examine their "selves" to learn about and understand their own beliefs and teaching strategies before attempting to understand their pupils ("the other"). Indeed, the metaphor of cyclical and reciprocal examination is apt here. Moreover, this model is reminiscent of the notion of reflexive inquiry described figuratively by Cole and Knowles (2000) in terms of mirrors and transparent prisms in which the various components are refracted, enlarged or broken down into the different colors of the spectrum.

I believe it would be advantageous for teacher education policymakers to consider the benefits of self-study when planning teacher education curricula and when providing or recommending continuing teacher education throughout the professional lives of teachers. Policymakers would also find it valuable to utilize teachers' insights and accumulated knowledge, gained through their own studies, when designing teacher education curricula and policy.

As is evident from the cases outlined in this book, teacher-inquirers can learn valuable lessons from self-study and as a result can move ahead with renewed confidence to the continuation of their professional lives as teachers. In fact, some teachers can even move on and liberate themselves from "old baggage" which often impeded them from progressing in their careers.

It appears that by examining cases in teaching practice through the lens of research, teacher-inquirers can learn significantly more than by implementing new courses of action based on intuition alone. The fable presented here can perhaps shed further light on the notion that teachers should be engaged in self-study in order to gain new on-the-job insights throughout their professional lives.

A nervous hare was sitting under a tree one morning when an enormous piece of fruit fell down from the tree and made the whole earth shake. "Earthquake!" he shouted and said, "Run for your lives!" as he raced off across the fields to warn his cousins. Other members of the hare family joined him and all hurried across the fields and up into the mountains in order to warn still more cousins as they ran. When they reached the top of the mountain, a wise lion asked them what had happened. "An earthquake," they said and he said, "Who saw the earthquake?" Then the hare led the wise lion down from the mountains and back across the fields to the place where he had been sitting under the tree. There the lion spotted the enormously large piece of fruit. He picked it up and then dropped it back down on the ground. It made a great big noise, but apart from that, nothing happened. "Oh," whispered the hare, "It wasn't an earthquake after all, was it?" The wise lion smiled kindly. "Never mind," he said. "All of us sometimes fear things we cannot understand." [28]

This story is a parable of how we as educators often operate in the teaching profession. Often we reach conclusions based on a single case, and frequently we act on the basis of feelings rather than attempting to understand the core and essence of matters in our decision-making process. Moreover, when we researchers present our research findings, someone from the audience is liable to respond by saying, "But we all know that." True, many matters are recognized as obvious or accepted truths, but these accepted truths are the fruit of idiosyncratic intuition. Through systematic and knowledge-based research, the researcher and the research community can obtain structured knowledge anchored in research evidence. Methodical and disciplined analysis of instructional situations, the teaching process and the professional life of a teacher allow teacher-inquirers to get to the root of matters and not be forced to act upon spontaneous gut feelings alone. Ultimately, then, our professional judgment will be based upon evidence. Our reasoning and assessment will be grounded in the findings of our research, carried out by means of the three approaches we have examined here: systematic and disciplined analysis of instructional situations and teaching practice, critical autobiography, and action research. Indeed, our research will enable us to anticipate the next stage in our teaching lives. Based upon our "expected cases of teaching" we will be capable of acting and reacting to new conditions, thereby continuing to grow and develop professionally.

NOTES

[1] Sagi, A. (2006). Hamassa hayehudi-israeli: Shelot shel tarbut vezehut [The Jewish-Israeli voyage: Culture and identity]. Jerusalem: The Shalom Hartman Institute.

[2] M.Ed. program at Levinsky College of Education in Israel.

[3] Labov (1972) proposed the term "evaluation devices" to describe the storyteller's point of view by signaling and establishing the various aspects of the 'point' of the story and of certain passages in the story.

[4] This is the original title the teacher-inquirers gave to their work. The story was told by Hagit Uzan and Michal Wertheimer in the Instructional Situations Analysis course in the M.Ed. graduate program on Learning and Instruction. The authentic and expected cases are presented here on their behalf and in their words.

[5] In Hebrew the teacher-inquirers titled their research work *"Aliya v'Kotz Bah?"* which literally means "Is there a thorn in immigration to Israel?" This is a deliberate misspelling of the original Hebrew expression "al'ya v'kotz bah," an idiom meaning "a mixed blessing," "a catch" or "a fly in the ointment." In the original Hebrew idiom, the word *"al'ya"* is written beginning with the letter *aleph*. The word *"aliya"* beginning with the letter *ayin* means "immigration to Israel". Hence, the deliberate misspelling reflects the two themes of the story, the importance of immigration to Israel and its concomitant problems.

[6] The teacher involved in the described case and her research partner were both students in the graduate program on Learning and Instruction. They both gave their approval to use material from their research but asked to remain anonymous. Therefore, their names are not mentioned. The authentic and expected case stories are presented here as written by the teacher-inquirers.

[7] In Israel, some schools implement an early childhood unit for children ages 4-8.

[8] The three question marks appear in the original, and they also serve the narrator as a means of evaluation.

[9] The authentic and expected cases are told by two teacher-inquirers who participated in the Instructional Situations Analysis course in the M.Ed. graduate program on Learning and Instruction. The teacher-inquirers have approved using the cases, which are presented here on their behalf and in their words. They wished to remain anonymous, that is why their names are not mentioned.

[10] A fictitious name.

[11] The quotation is taken from a poem by Israeli poet Natan Zach, "Ani rotseh tamid einayim" [I Always Want Eyes]. The poem is a prayerful poem declaring the beauty of the world.

[12] Perceived self-efficacy is defined as people's beliefs about their capabilities to produce designated levels of performance that exercise influence over events that affect their lives. Self-efficacy beliefs determine how people feel, think, motivate themselves and behave (Bandura, 1994).

[13] The grade is 80% out of 100%, equivalent to a grade of B.

[14] The English class described in this story is English as a Foreign Language, a compulsory subject taught in the Israeli schools from the 4th to the 12th grades.

[15] Zach, N. (1971). *"Ani Tamid Rotze Einaim"* ["I Always Want Eyes"], *Kol Hachalav Vehadvash [All the Milk and Honey]*. Tel Aviv: Am Oved Publishers, p. 20.

[16] http://www.amazon.com/gp/reader/0671617680/ref=sib_dp_pt#reader-link

[17] Through this grammatical error, the writer seeks to show that the pupil speaks incorrect English.

[18] http://www.amazon.com/gp/reader/0743243773/ref=sib_dp_pt#reader-link

[19] The examples in this section are taken from Idit Friedman's self-study: Friedman, I. (2006). In spite of and regardless of everything - a teacher. The story of my life as a key to understanding my professional development in teaching multicultural classes. Thesis, submitted to the M.Ed. program on Language Education in a Multicultural Society, Levinsky College of Education.

[20] In Israel, women are recruited into the army at age 18 to do eighteen months of compulsory service.

[21] Stories from the past are printed in italics.

22 In writing about mending things, Idit uses the Hebrew word *tikkun*. *Tikkun* is a mystical Jewish Cabbalistic concept, which literally means "to mend" or "to repair," usually in the context of fixing the world. In Hebrew, the word *tikkun* is usually used as a figure of speech to express a kind of mystical and just "mending" or "repairing" of one's own life.

23 These examples are taken from Galit Attal's self-study: Attal, G. (2008*). A Journey to Myself— From my Kibbutz Childhood until Today.* Paper submitted to a seminar course on Multiculturalism and Multilingualism in a Multicultural society in the M.Ed program on Language Education in a Multicultural Society, Levinsky College of Education.

24 "The kibbutz (Hebrew word for 'communal settlement') is a unique rural community; a society dedicated to mutual aid and social justice; a socioeconomic system based on the principle of joint ownership of property, equality and cooperation of production, consumption and education; the fulfillment of the idea 'from each according to his ability, to each according to his needs'; a home for those who have chosen it."
(Source: http://www.jewishvirtuallibrary.org/jsource/Society_&_Culture/kibbutz.html)

25 "Hashomer Hatza'ir - (Hebrew – 'The Young Guard') is a Marxist Zionist youth movement, founded in Europe in 1916, to prepare Jewish youth for kibbutz life in Israel. In addition to Zionism, its ideology meshes Jewish culture with scouting and youth values. It is affiliated with the Kibbutz Artzi movement today. Hashomer Hatzair spawned the Mapam Party and the Kibbutzim of the Kibbutz Artzi."
(Source: http://www.zionism-israel.com/dic/Hashomer_Hatzair.htm)

26 The examples are taken from Mali Yitzhak's self-study: Yitzhak, M. (2008). *Language Arts Education – Education for Life*, a paper submitted during a research seminar in the M.Ed. program on Language Education in a Multicultural Society.

27 A fictitious name.

28 The story, Hare Heralds the Earthquake, by Rosalind Kerven, appeared on the PIRLS international examination for fourth graders in 2001. The text as it appears here is condensed and has been rewritten by me for the purposes of this discussion and summary.

BIBLIOGRAPHY

Ashton-Warner, S. (1963). *Teacher*. New York: Simon and Schuster.

Bamberg, M. (2006). Stories: Big or small. Why do we care? *Narrative Inquiry, 16*(1), 139–147.

Bandura, A. (1994). Self-efficacy. In V. S. Ramachaudran (Ed.), *Encyclopedia of Human Behavior* (Vol. 4, pp. 71–81). New York: Academic Press.

Bass, L., Anderson-Patton, V., & Allender, J. (2002). Self-study as a way of teaching and learning. In J. Loughran & T. Russell (Eds.), *Improving teacher education practice through self-study*. London: RoutledgeFalmer.

Beijaard, D., Verloop, N., & Vermunt, J. D. (2000). Teachers' perceptions of professional identity: An exploratory study from a personal knowledge perspective. *Teaching and Teacher Education, 16*, 749–764.

Beijaard, D. (1995). Teachers' prior experiences and actual perceptions of professional identity. *Teachers and Teaching: Theory and Practice, 1*, 281–294.

Benesch, S. (1993). ESL authors and writing critical autobiographies. In J. Carson & I. Leki (Eds.), *Reading in the composition classroom* (pp. 247–257). Boston: Heinle and Henle.

Berry, A. (2004). Self-study in teaching about teaching. In J. Loughran, M. L. Hamilton, V. LaBoskey, & T. Russell (Eds.), *International handbook of self-study of teaching and teacher education practices* (Vol. 2, pp. 1295–1332). Dordrecht, The Netherlands: Kluwer Academic.

Berry, A., & Loughran, J. (2005). Teaching about teaching, the role of self study. In C. Mitchell, S. Weber, & K. O'Reilly-Scanlon (Eds.), *Just who do we think we are? Methodologies for autobiography and self-study in teaching* (pp. 167–180). London and New York: RouteldgeFalmer, Taylor & Francis Group.

Bloom, L. R., & Munro, P. (1995). Conflicts: Non-unitary subjectivity in women administrator's life history narratives. In J. A. Hatch & R. Wisniewski (Eds.), *Life History and Narrative* (pp. 99–112). London: Falmer Press.

Borko, H., Whitcomb, J. A., & Byrnes, K. (2008). Genres of research in teacher education. In M. Cochran-Smith, S. Feiman-Nemser, D. J. McIntyre, & K. E. Demers (Eds.), *Handbook of research on teacher education* (pp. 1017–1049). New York and London: Routledge, Taylor & Francis Group.

Bryman, A. (2006). Integrating quantitative and qualitative research: How is it done? *Qualitative Research, 6*(1), 97–113.

Bullough, R. V., & Pinnegar, S. (2001). Guidelines for quality in autobiographical forms of self-study research. *Educational Researcher, 30*(3), 13–21.

Bullough, R. V., & Pinnegar, S. (2004). Thinking about the thinking about self-study: An analysis of eight chapters. In J. Loughran, M. L. Hamilton, V. LaBoskey, & T. Russell (Eds.), *International handbook of self-study of teaching and teacher education practices* (Vol. 2, pp. 313–342). Dordrecht, The Netherlands: Kluwer Academic.

Burbules, N. (1993). *Dialogue in teaching: Theory and practice*. New York: Teachers College Press.

Burkhardt, H., & Schoenfeld, A. H. (2003). Improving educational research: Toward a more useful, more influential, and better-funded enterprise. *Educational Researcher, 32*(9), 3–14.

Carr, W., & Kemmis, S. (1986). *Becoming critical: Education, knowledge & action Research*. London: Falmer Press.

Carter, K. (1999). What is a case? What is not a case? In M. A. Lundeberg, B. B. Levin, & H. L. Harrington (Eds.), *Who learns what from cases and how? The research base for teaching and learning with cases* (pp. 165–175). Mahwah, NJ: Lawrence Erlbaum Associates, Publishers.

Clandinin, D. J., & Connelly, F. M. (2000). *Narrative inquiry: Experience and story in qualitative research*. San Francisco: Jossey-Bass Publishers.

Clements, P. (1999). Autobiographical research and the emergence of the fictive voice. *Cambridge Journal of Education, 29*(1), 21–32.

Cochran-Smith, M., & Lytle, S. (1993). *Inside/outside: Teacher research and knowledge.* New York: Teachers College Press.

Cohen, L., Manion, L., & Morrison, K. (2007). *Research methods in education.* London and New York: Routledge, Taylor Francis Group.

Cole, A. L., & Knowles, J. G. (2000). *Researching teaching: Exploring teacher development through reflexive inquiry.* MA: Allyn & Bacon.

Craig, C. J. (2006). Why is dissemination so difficult? The nature of teacher knowledge and the spread of curriculum reform. *American Educational Research Journal, 43*(2), 157–293.

Creswell, J. W. (1998). *Qualitative inquiry and research design; Choosing among five traditions.* Sage Publications.

Denzin, N. K. (2008). The new paradigm dialogs and qualitative inquiry. *International Journal of Qualitative Studies in Education, 21*(4), 315–325.

Dinkelman, T. (2003). Self-study in teacher education – A means and ends tool for promoting reflective teaching. *Journal of Teacher Education, 54*(1), 6–18.

Doecke, B. (2004). Professional identity and educational reform: Confronting my habitual practices as a teacher educator. *Teaching and Teacher Education, 20*, 203–215.

Elbaz-Luwisch, F. (2005). *Teacher's voices: Storytelling and possibility.* Greenwich, CT: Information Age Publishing.

Evans, L. (2002). *Reflective practice in educational research: Developing advanced skills.* London: Continuum.

Ezer, H. (1998). Dialog mafre behanchaya reflectivit – emzai leha'azama wuleshinuy bsis hayeda [Inspired dialogue in reflective instruction as a means of empowerment and changing the knowledge base]. In M. Silberstein, M. Ben-Peretz, & S. Ziv (Eds.), *Reflekzia behora'a - zir merkazi behitpatchut hamore [Reflection in teaching – A central axis in teacher development]* (pp. 303–323). Tel-Aviv: Mofet Institute.

Ezer, H. (2002a). Hanchayat diyun besipurey hora'a shel morim le'oryanut [Discussion mentoring in the instructional cases of literacy teachers]. In P. Katz & M. Silberstein (Eds.), *Eruey hadracha ve'eruey hora'a: pedagogia shel sifrut mikrim behachsharat morim [Mentoring and teaching events: Pedagogy of case literature in teacher education]* (pp. 176–196). Tel-Aviv: Mofet Institute Publications.

Ezer, H. (2002b). *Tipuach hitnahaguyot oryaniot etzel yeled mitkashe: sipura shel hamora Ayelet* [Promoting literacy behaviors in a special needs pupil: The story of Ayelet, the teacher]. In P. Katz & M. Silberstein (Eds.), *Eruey hadracha ve'eruey hora'a: pedagogia shel sifrut mikrim behachsharat morim [Mentoring and teaching events: Pedagogy of case literature in teacher education]* (pp. 388–411). Tel-Aviv: Mofet Institute Publications.

Ezer, H. (2004). *Rav tarbutiyut bachevra wubeveit hassefer: Hebetim chinuchiyim ve'oryaniyim* [Multiculturalism in society and in school: Educational and literacy considerations]. Ra'anana: The Open University.

Ezer, H., & Mevorach, M. (2008). Shinuy ba'irgun hachinuch: Hasipur hamezupe, hamuzhar ve'hanitpas [Changes in educational organization: The expected, declared and perceived story]. Research report. Research, Evaluation and Development Authority, Levinsky College of Education.

Ezer, H., Millet, S., & Patkin, D. (2005). Voices of multicultural experiences: Personal narratives of three teacher educators. *Teacher Education and Practice, 18*(1), 55–73.

Feiman-Nemser, S. (2001). From preparation to practice: Designing a continuum to strengthen and sustain teaching. *Teachers College Record, 103*(6), 335–348.

Feldman, A. (2003). Validity and quality in self-study. *Educational Researcher, 3*(3), 26–28.

Flores, M. A., & Day, C. (2006). Contexts which shape and reshape new teachers' identities: A multi-perspective study. *Teaching and Teacher Education, 22*, 219–232.

Freeman, M. (2007). Autobiographical understanding and narrative inquiry. In D. J. Clandinin (Ed.), *Handbook of narrative inquiry mapping a methodology* (pp. 120–145). Thousand Oaks, CA: Sage Publications.

Freire, P. (1996). *Letters to Christina. Reflections on my life and work.* New York and London: Routledge.

Gee, J. P. (1992). *The Social mind: Language, ideology and social practice.* New York: Bergin & Garvey.

Gee, J. P. (1999). *An introduction to discourse analysis: Theory and method.* London: Routledge.

Georgakopolou, A., & Goutsos, D. (1999). *Discourse analysis, an introduction.* Edinburgh: Edinburgh University Press.

Goldblatt, P. F., & Smith, D. (2004). Illuminating and facilitating professional knowledge through case work. *European Journal of Teacher Education, 27*(3), 335–354.

Goldblatt, P. F., & Smith, D. (2005). *Cases for teacher development: Preparing for the classroom.* Thousand Oaks, CA: Sage Publications.

Goodnough, K. (2005). Issues in modified problem-based learning: A self-study in pre-service science-teacher education. *Canadian Journal of Sciences, Mathematics and Technology Education,* 289–305.

Goodson, I. F. (1992). Studying teachers' lives: An emergent field of inquiry. In F. Goodson (Ed.), *Studying teachers' lives* (pp. 1–17). London: Routledge.

Hacohen, R., & Zimran, I. (1999). *Mechkar pe'ula: Morim chokrim et avodatam* [Action research: Teachers researching their work]. Tel Aviv: Klil Press, Mofet Institute.

Harris, M. Y. (2005). Black women writing autobiography. In J. Phillion, M. Fang He, & F. M. Connelly (Eds.), *Narrative & experience in multicultural education* (pp. 36–52). Thousand Oaks, CA: Sage Publications.

Hartman, D. K. (1998). *Stories teachers tell: Reflecting on professional practice.* Lincolnwood, IL: National Textbook Company in conjunction with the Northeast Conference on the Teaching of Foreign Languages.

Hashweh, M. Z. (2004). Case-writing as border-crossing: Describing, explaining and promoting teacher change. *Teachers and Teaching: Theory and Practice, 10*(3), 229–246.

Hostetler, K. (2005). What is "good" education research? *Educational researcher, 34*(6), 16–21.

Hutchings, P., & Shulman, L. S. (1999). Find more like this: the scholarship of teaching. *Change, 31*(5), 10–16.

Johnstone, B. (2001). Discourse analysis and narrative. In D. Schiffrin, D. Tannen, & H. E. Hamilton (Eds.), *The handbook of discourse analysis* (pp. 635–649). Malden, MA: Blackwell Publishers Inc.

Karnieli, M. (2003). Keizad magdirim hazlacha bemechkar pe'ula? [How is success measured in action research?] In D. Levy (Ed.), *Mechkar pe'ula – halacha wuma'asse: Zikot filosofiot wumetodologiot bein mechkar pe'ula levein paradigmat hamechkar ha'eichuti [Action research – theory and practice: Philosophical and methodological relations between action research and the qualitative research paradigm]* (pp. 179–194). Tel Aviv: Mofet Institute.

Keiny, S. (2006). Mechkar pe'ula beveit hassefer – perek bet [Action research in school – Part 2]. *Chashiva ekologit – gisha chadasha leshinuy chinuchi [Ecological thinking: A new approach to educational change]* (pp. 41–66). Tel Aviv: Mofet Institute.

Kennedy, M. M. (1999). A test of some common contentions about educational research. *American Educational Research Journal, 36*(3), 511–541.

Ketelle, D. (2004). Writing truth as fiction: Administrators think about their work through a different lens. *The Qualitative Report, 9*(3), 449–462.

Kincheloe, J. L. (2003). Teachers as researchers: Qualitative inquiry as a path to empowerment (2nd ed.). New York: Routledge Farmer.

Kincheloe, J. L., & Tobin, K. (2006). Doing educational research in a complex world: Preface. In J. L. Kincheloe & K. Tobin (Eds.), *Doing educational research, a handbook* (pp. 3–14). Rotterdam/Taipei: Sense Publishers.

Kubler LaBoskey, V. (2005). Speak for yourselves, capturing the complexity of critical reflection. In C. Mitchell, S. Weber, & K. O'Reilly-Scanlon (Eds.), *Just who do we think we are? Methodologies for autobiography and self-study in teaching* (pp. 131–141). London and New York: RouteldgeFalmer, Taylor & Francis Group.

Kupferberg, I., & Gilat, I. (2002). *Gsharim metaphoriyim narrativiyim betikshoret bein ishit* [Metaphorical-narrative bridges in interpersonal communication]. Tel Aviv: Mofet Institute.

Labov, W. (1972). *Language in the city: Studies in the Black English vernacular.* Philadelphia: University of Pennsylvania Press.

Linde, C. (2001). Narrative in institutions. In D. Schiffrin, D. Tannen, & H. E. Hamilton (Eds.), *The handbook of discourse analysis* (pp. 518–535). Malden, MA: Blackwell Publishers, Inc.

Loewenberg Ball, D., & Forzani, M. (2007). What makes education research "educational"? *Educational Researcher, 36*(9), 529–540.

Loughran, J. (2007). Researching teacher education practices: Responding to the challenges, demands, and expectations of self-study. *Journal of Teacher Education, 58*(1), 12–20.

Luke, A. (2004). Theory and practice in critical discourse analysis. In L. Saha (Ed.), *International Encyclopedia of the Sociology of Education.* Elsevier Science Ltd.

Lundeberg, M. A. (1999). Discovering teaching and learning through cases. In M. A. Lundeberg, B. B. Levin, & H. L. Harrington (Eds.), *Who learns what from cases and how? The research base for teaching and learning with cases* (pp. 3–27). Mahwah, NJ: Lawrence Erlbaum Associates, Publishers.

Lundeberg, M. A., Levin, B. B., & Harrington, H. L. (1999). *Who learns what from cases and how? The research base for teaching and learning with cases.* Mahwah, NJ: Lawrence Erlbaum Associates, Publishers.

Lyons, N., & Kubler LaBoskey, V. (2002). Introduction. In N. Lyons & V. Kubler LaBoskey (Eds.), *Narrative inquiry in practice* (pp. 1–10). New York: Teachers College Press.

Maclure, M. (1993). Arguing for yourself: Identity as an organizing principle in teachers' jobs and lives. *British Educational Research Journal, 19*(4), 311–322.

Margolin, I., Ezer, H., & Silberstein, M. (2001). Pituach chashiva reflectivit bemahalch hamashov hapedagogi: Sipur mikre wumodel lenitucho [Developing reflective thinking from pedagogical feedback: The "case story" and a model for its analysis]. In R. Zuzovsky, T. Ariav, & A. Keinan (Eds.), *Hachsharat morim vehitpatchutam hamikzoit:Chilufei ra'ayonot [The ongoing development of teacher education: Exchange of ideas]* (pp. 135–153). Tel Aviv: Mofet Institute.

McCourt, F. (2005). *Teacher man: A memoire.* New York: Scribner.

McLaughlin, C., Black-Hawkins, K., McIntyre, D., & Townsend, A. (2008). *Networking practitioner research.* London and New York: Routledge, Taylor & Francis Group.

McNiff, J., & Whitehead, J. (2002). *Action research: Principles and practice* (2nd ed.). London: RouteledgeFalmer.

Merseth, K. K. (1999). Foreword: A rationale for case-based pedagogy in teacher education. In M. A. Lundeberg, B. B. Levin, & H. L. Harrington (Eds.), *Who learns what from cases and how? The research base for teaching and learning with cases* (pp. ix–xv). Mahwah, NJ: Lawrence Erlbaum Associates, Publishers.

Meyer, J. R. (1996). *Stories from the heart: Teachers and students researching their literacy lives.* NJ: Lawrence Erlbaum Associates, Publishers.

Mitchell, C., & Weber, S. (2005). Just who do we think we are … and how do we know this? Re-visioning pedagogical spaces for studying our teaching selves. In C. Mitchell, S. Weber, & K. O'Reilly-Scanlon (Eds.), *Just who do we think we are? Methodologies for autobiography and self-study in teaching* (pp. 1–9). London and New York: RouteldgeFalmer, Taylor & Francis Group.

Mooney, R. (1957). *Research for curriculum improvement, association of supervision and curriculum development.* Washington, DC: Association of Curriculum Development.

Mueller, A. (2003). Looking back and looking forward: Always becoming a teacher educator through self-study. *Reflective Practice, 4*(1), 67–84.

Nias, J. (1989). Teaching and the self. In M. L. Holly & C. S McLoughlin (Eds.), *Perspective on teacher professional development* (pp. 151–171). London: Falmer Press.

Nieto, S. (1999). *The light in their eyes: Creating multicultural learning communities.* NY: Teachers College, Columbia University.

Onwuegbuzie, A. J., Witcher, A. E., Collins, K. M. T., Filer, J. D. Wiedmaier, C. D., & Moore, C. W. (2007). Students' perceptions of characteristics of effective college teachers: A validity study of a teaching evaluation form using a mixed methods analysis. *American Educational Research Journal, 44*(1), 113–160.

Paulus, T. M., Woodside, M., & Ziegler, M. (2007). "Determined women at work". Group construction of narrative meaning. *Narrative Inquiry, 17*(2), 299–328.

Pinnegar, S. (1998). Methodological perspectives: Introduction. In M. L. Hamilton (Ed.), *Reconceptualizing teaching practice: Self-study in teacher education* (pp. 31–33). London: Falmer.

Roberts-Holmes, G. (2003). Towards an understanding of Gambian teachers' complex professionalism. *Teachers and Teaching: Theory and Practice, 9*(1), 35–44.

Robinson, J. A., & Taylor, L. R. (1998). Autobiographical memory and self-narratives: A tale of two stories. In C. P. Thompson, D. J. Herrmann, D. Bruce, J. D. Read, D. G. Payne & M. P. Toglia (Eds.), *Autobiographical memory, theoretical and applied perspectives* (pp. 125–143). Mahwah, NJ: Lawrence Erlbaum Associates, Publishers.

Robinson, M., & McMillan, W. (2006). Who teaches the teachers? Identity, discourse and policy in teacher education. *Teaching and Teacher Education, 22,* 327–336.

Rodgers, C. R., & Scott, K. H. (2008). The development of the personal self and professional identity in learning to teach. In M. Cochran-Smith, S. Feiman-Nemser, D. J. McIntyre, & K. E. Demers (Eds.), *Handbook of research on teacher education/Enduring questions in changing contexts* (3rd ed., pp. 732–755). New York and London: Routledge.

Russell, T. (2006). How 20 years of self-study changed my teaching. In C. Kosnik, C. Beck, A. R. Freese, & A. P. Samaras (Eds.), *Making a difference in teacher education through self-study: Studies of persona, professional and program renewal* (pp. 3–18). Dordrecht, The Netherlands: Springer.

Sabar Ben-Yehoshua, N. (1990). *Hmechkar ha'eichuti ba'ora'a wubalemida* [Qualitative Research in Teaching and Learning]. Tel-Aviv: Massada Press.

Sabar Ben-Yehoshua, N. (Ed.). (2001). *Massorot wuzramim bamechkar ha'eichuti* [Genres and tradition in qualitative research]. Tel Aviv: Dvir.

Schiffrin, D., Tannen, D., & Hamilton, H. E. (2001). Introduction. In D. Schiffrin, D. Tannen, & H. E. Hamilton (Eds.), *The handbook of discourse analysis* (pp. 1–10). Malden, MA: Blackwell Publishers Inc.

Sharkey, J. (2004). Lives stories don't tell: Exploring the untold in autobiographies. *Curriculum Inquiry, 34*(4), 495–512.

Shor, I., & Freire, P. (1987). *A pedagogy for liberation: Dialogues on transforming education.* South Hadley, MA: Bergin & Garvey Publishers.

Shkedi, A. (2004). *Milim shemenassot laga'at: Mechkar eichutani – te'orya ve'yissum* [Words of meanings: Qualitative research – theory and practice]. Tel Aviv: Ramot, Tel-Aviv University.

Shulman, J. (1996). Tender feelings, hidden thoughts: Confronting bias, innocence and racism through case discussions. In J. Colbert, P. Desberg, & K. Trimple (Eds.), *The case for education: Contemporary approaches for using case methods* (pp. 137–158). Boston: Allyn & Bacon.

Shulman, L. S. (1986). Those who understand: Knowledge growth in teaching. *Educational Researcher, 15*(2), 4–14.

Silberstein, M. (1998). Mavo [Introduction]. In M. Silberstein, M. Ben-Peretz, & S. Ziv (Eds.), *Reflekzia be'hora'a – zir merkazi be'hitpatchut more [Reflection in teaching – A central axis in teacher development]* (pp. 5–14). Tel Aviv: Mofet Institute.

Silberstein, M. (2002). Mekoma shel sifrut mikrim betochniot hahachshara shel morim [The place of case literature in teacher education programs]. In P. Katz & M. Silberstein (Eds.), *Eruey hadracha ve'eruey hora'a: pedagogia shel sifrut mikrim behachsharat morim [Mentoring and teaching events: pedagogy of case literature in teacher education]* (pp. 6–36). Tel-Aviv: Mofet Institute.

Tashakkori, A., & Teddlie, C. (2008). The evolution of mixed methods research. In V.L. Plano Clark & J. W. Creswell (2008). *The mixed methods reader* (pp. 7–26). California: Sage Publications, Inc.

Teddlie, C., & Tashakkori, A. (2003). Major issues and controversies in the use of mixed methods in the social and behavioral sciences. In A. Tashakkori & C. Teddlie (Eds.), *Handbook of mixed methods in social & behavioral research* (pp. 3–50). Thousand Oaks, CA: Sage Publications.

Van Dijk, T. A. (2001). Discourse analysis and narrative. In D. Schiffrin, D. Tannen, & H. E. Hamilton (Eds.), *The handbook of discourse analysis* (pp.352–371). Malden, MA: Blackwell Publishers Inc.

Van Manen, M. (1980). An interview with a Dutch pedagogue. *Journal of Curriculum Theorizing, 2*(2), 68–72.

Vygotsky, L. S. (1962). *Thought and language*. Cambridge: MIT Press.

Vygotsky, L. S. (1978). *Mind in society: The development of higher psychological processes*. Cambridge: Harvard University Press.

Whitehead, J. (1993). *The growth of educational knowledge: Creating your own living educational theories*. Bournemouth, UK: Hyde Publications.

Zeichner, K. (1999). The new scholarship in teacher education. *Educational Researcher, 28*(9), 4–15.

Zeichner, K. M. (2005). A research agenda for teacher education. In M. Cochran-Smith & K. M. Zeichner, (Eds.), *Studying teacher education: The report of the AERA panel on research and teacher education* (pp. 737–759). Washington, DC: AERA-American Educational Research Association, Mahwah, NJ: LEA - Lawrence Erlbaum Associates, Publishers.

Zeichner, K. M., & Konklin, H. G. (2005). Teacher education programs. In M. Chocran-Smith & K. M. Zeichner (Eds.), *Studying teacher education: The report of the AERA panel on research and teacher education* (pp. 645–735). Washington, DC: AERA-American Educational Research Association; Mahwah, NJ: LEA - Lawrence Erlbaum Associates, Publishers.

Zellermayer, M., & Keiny, S. (2006). Ha'azmi beyachas la'acherim bemechkar pe'ula [The "self" with regard to others in action research]. In D. Levy (Ed.), *Mechkar pe'ula – halacha wuma'asse: Zikot filosofiot wumetodologiot bein mechkar pe'ula levein paradigmat hamechkar ha'eichuti [Action research – theory and practice: Philosophical and methodological relations between action research and the qualitative research paradigm]* (pp. 83–102). Tel-Aviv: Mofet Institute.

Zellermayer, M., & Tabak, E. (2004). *"Anachnu naasse et ze beinenu" o: eich mechkar pe'ula bone ke'hila mikzo'it lomedet bemisgeret shel amitut michlala-sade* ["We shall do it among ourselves" or: how does action research construct learning professional community in a school-college partnership?]. Tel-Aviv: Mofet Institute.

Zeni, J. (2001). Introduction. In J. Zeni (Ed.), *Ethical issues in practitioner research* (pp. xi–xxi). New York: Teachers College, Columbia University.

ABOUT THE AUTHOR

Dr. Hanna Ezer is currently head of Research & Development at Levinsky College of Education in Israel. She previously served as Director of Academic Studies and as a member of the board at the college. She is a graduate of the Department of Bilingual Education at Boston University School of Education, USA. Her current research focuses on processes in teacher education, multiculturalism in education and teacher education, and conceptualization of academic writing in different cultural groups of teachers and of students.

INDEX

Printed in the United States
By Bookmasters